CAMDEN TOWN AND PRIMROSE HILL PAST

First published 1991
Reprinted 2002
by Historical Publications Ltd
32 Ellington Street, London N7 8PL
(Tel: 020 7607 1628)

ISBN 0 948667 12 5
British Library Cataloguing-in-Publication Data
A catalogue record for this book is available from the British Library

Typeset in Palatino by Historical Publications Ltd
Reproduction by G & J Graphics, London EC2
Printed by South China Printing Company, Hong Kong

CAMDEN TOWN
AND PRIMROSE HILL
PAST

John Richardson

HISTORICAL PUBLICATIONS

Acknowledgements

I have received enthusiastic help from many quarters. In particular the assistance of Roger Cline, Lester May and Basil Leverton has been frequent and invaluable.

I should also like to thank the following: Malcolm Holmes, Valerie Hart, Richard Knight and Lesley Marshall of the Local Studies Library of the London Borough of Camden; Graham Barrett of Lawford's; Keith Bird and Harriet Garland of the Arlington Action Group; John Dickinson; Barry Hales of the Regent Pet Stores; Ivor Leverton; Rachel Priestman of Northside UK; Mrs Romany; Fred Russell; John Saxby of Montagu Saxby; Jinny Schiele; Stephen Simmonds; Gillian Tindall; Linda Warden and Jane Kingsley at the Royal Veterinary College.

The Illustrations

The following have kindly given their permission for illustrations to be reproduced:

The British Council: 84

The London Borough of Camden: 7, 8, 13, 15, 16, 19, 24, 25, 35, 36, 41, 43, 47, 52, 62, 63, 73, 75, 76, 86, 87, 92, 97, 98, 100, 102, 105, 106, 109, 110, 117, 119, 121, 122, 127, 131, 133, 135, 137, 138, 139, 140, 141, 144, 145

Roger Cline: 45, 50, 51, 95, 132, 142

John Dickinson: 141

International Distillers and Vintners: 44

Richard Lansdown: 129

Lawford's: 103, 114, 115, 116

Leverton & Sons Ltd: 82, 112

Lester May: 74, 78

National Portrait Gallery: 90

Northside Developments: 23, 152

The Pirate's Castle Club: 149

Mrs Romany: 126

Royal Veterinary College: 26, 27, 28, 29, 128

Fred Russell: 113

The jacket illustration is of *The Railway over the Canal at Camden Town*, by T.T. Bury, published by Ackermann in 1837. It is reproduced by kind permission of the London Borough of Camden.

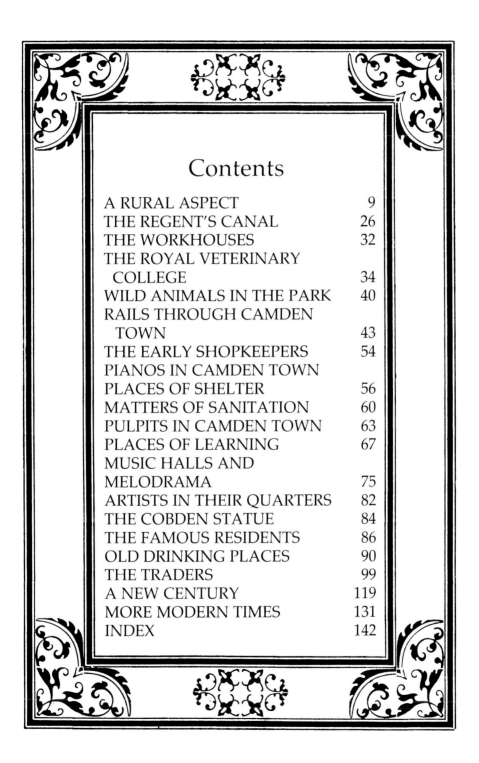

Contents

Further Reading

Bordass, M.E.E., *Primrose Hill Studios 1877–83*, unpub. (1981?) (copy at Camden Local Studies Library).

Camden History Society, *Camden History Review*, various editions.

Cline, Roger, *Regent's Park and Primrose Hill*, unpub. dissertation (1991).

Cooper, Anthony (ed), Primrose Hill to Euston Road (rev. 1984).

Cotchin, Prof. Ernest, *The Royal Veterinary College London* (1991).

Country Life, Old Euston (1938).

Flood, Aidan, *The Irish in Camden* (1991).

Hassiotis, Anna, *The Greek Cypriot Community in Camden* (1991).

London County Council, *Survey of London, Vol. XIX, St Pancras pt II* (1938).

London Topographical Society, *The Kentish Town Panorama* (facsimile reproduction 1986), drawings by James King, commentary by John Richardson.

Miller, Frederick, *St Pancras Past and Present* (1874).

Mitchell, P. Chalmers, *Centenary History of the Zoological Society of London* (1929).

Nelson, Sarah, *The History of the Camden Goods Yard*, unpub. article 1986 (copy at Camden Local Studies Library).

Rottman, Alex, *London Catholic Churches* (1926).

Saunders, Ann, *Regent's Park* (1969).

Schiele, Jinny, *Post-war Theatre in Camden: a Study of three theatre enterprises (The Bedford, Open Space and Roundhouse 1949–83)*, unpub. thesis (1987), Polytechnic of North London.

Scott Rogers, Jean, *A Short History of St Mark's Church* (1978).

Scrimgeour, R.M. (ed), *The North London Collegiate School* (1950).

Sheridan, Michael, *Rowton Houses 1892–1954* (1956).

Tindall, Gillian, *The Fields Beneath* (1977).

Introduction

Few places in London can be so precise as Camden Town about its origins. In 1791, what was previously a hinterland of Kentish Town, a junction of roads to Hampstead and Highgate, with two pubs and a few houses, obtained a fresh name even before many buildings were above foundation level. Development was slow, uncertain and of indifferent quality: it was not a good beginning. Even that totem of respectability, an Anglican church, which marked an area either as a potential or actual success, did not appear until over thirty years later.

Chalk Farm came later still. The Chalk Farm Tavern existed in 1791, an isolated house on the lane which became Regent's Park Road, but not much else. And just as development was about to begin nearby the railway intruded and delayed the process.

As it happens much of what was first built in both areas still survives. The most notable exception is the High Street, where nothing of the first main road appears to be left. The High Street, in fact, is almost devoid of architectural distinction, save the Camden Theatre, the old Bowman building and the Mother Black Cap. It is a dispiriting range of buildings as though to underline that the function of the passer-by was not to admire the scenery but to keep his or her eyes down to examine the prices on the merchandise.

The shops were and still are the most influential aspect of Camden Town, and in its 200th year, after a period of decline, the area is reasserting itself as the major retail centre for north London.

This collection of illustrations has been culled from many sources in an attempt to portray the area from its rural state to quite modern times. Pictures of the Camden Town area are hard to come by. Apart from Primrose Hill, it was not pretty and until the advent of the Camden Town Group of painters it was virtually ignored by artists. And, like Kentish Town, in the boom time of picture postcards Camden Town warranted only black and white views. Unfortunately, Sickert, who liked Camden Town, spent too much time drawing the interior scenes in the Bedford and not enough painting the streets of naphtha lamps. In fact the most prolific artist of Camden Town was the photographer hired by the underground railway to capture in detail each building along the proposed route.

One quality which I think is common to many of the illustrations, is energy and movement. It is not a sleepy town, it is not pretty, it is not quaint, it is not suburban. But it is a place where patterns change, things get done, and new circumstances are faced. In its 200th year Camden Town is still lively.

John Richardson 1991

1. Rocque's map of the St Pancras and Camden Town area in c1746. Fig Lane is now Crowndale Road.

2. *At Mother Red Caps on the road to Hampstead*, by Samuel Hieronymous Grimm, 1772. The view is to the south and, presumably, the building on the right is the Mother Black Cap, later to be converted into the St Pancras Workhouse.

A Rural Aspect

LORD CAMDEN'S FIELDS

Camden Town is a new name, at least by London standards. About 1791 the 1st Earl of Camden, Charles Pratt, let out some plots of land on the eastern side of the High Street, and in the same year an isolated sprawl in the London countryside was dignified by the name of Camden Town.

In truth, the area had no proper designation before, a fact underlined in 1788 when building permission was granted to Camden embodied in a 'Kentish Town Act'. Not much more than fields lay between Somers Town and Euston Road to the south and the village of Kentish Town to the north. At this period the fields were known, at least to the man drawing up the first parish map soon after, rather prosaically for the most part by the number of acres they contained, although there is an occasional name reminding us of either past crops or owners, such as Figs Meadow.

Quite often the area of today's Camden Town underground station was called Halfway Houses, indicating not only a mid-point between St Giles's Circus and Hampstead or Highgate but the presence of two public houses, the Mother Black Cap and the Mother Red Cap; the Rocque map of mid–18th century uses just the latter pub name for the road junction here. Early prints of the Mother Red Cap depict a business that just scraped by: bereft of customers in the immediate vicinity it stole passing trade that could not wait to get further along the road. The status of this area is summed up in earlier decisions to erect, first, some gallows and, later, a workhouse on the site of the station.

The western side of the High Street was Lord Southampton's land and there some fairly mean development with restricted site widths had taken place by 1791. Camden, on the other hand, laid out his buildings along the High Street to more generous proportions: that difference of shop frontage on the two sides of the road is still reflected today. Camden's lessees completed the triangle of houses immediately south of the Mother Red Cap first. They left, for some reason, the old Bowman's store

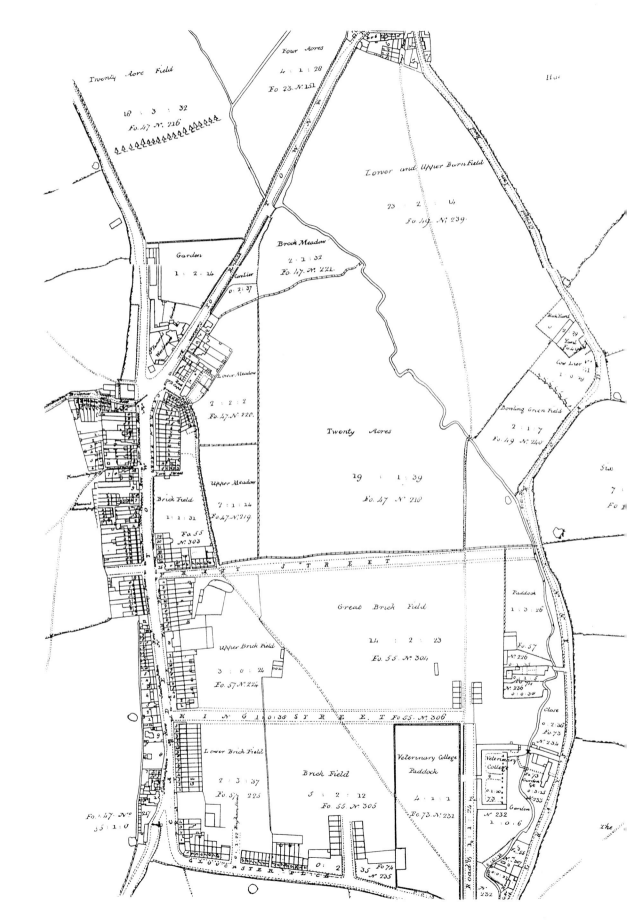

3. *Thompson's map of the St Pancras Parish, c1800,* Camden Town area. Development on both sides of the High Street, apart from the subsequent Bowman's site, has been completed and some roads in the hinterland have been laid out. At this time the Veterinary College had a paddock on the opposite side of the incipient Royal College Street.

4. *Charles Pratt, 1st Earl of Camden (1713–94).*

site empty, but then lined the street down to Crowndale Road. In the hinterland were laid out the routes of Pratt and Plender Streets and a lease was granted to the newly-founded Veterinary College in what became Royal College Street.

Some field names in that first parish survey bear testimony to the contemporary transition from agricultural to building land – Great Brick Field, Lower Brick Field, Upper Brick Field, and on the other side of the road Tile Kiln Field, all indicate the nature of Camden Town's soil and its new usefulness.

The 1st Earl of Camden, Charles Pratt, who gave his name to this new area of London, died in 1794. In fact, in a convoluted way, Camden Town derives its name not from him but from the famous 16th-century scholar and headmaster of Westminster School, William Camden, who retired to a house in Chislehurst, later called Camden Place, which Charles Pratt took as one of his residences and for his title. The Camden family supplied a number of street names. Pratt was married to Elizabeth Jeffreys, of Brecknock; another of his titles was Viscount Bayham (from Bayham Abbey). Two of his children were Georgiana and Caroline (Carol Street was once Caroline Street); his son, George, married Harriet Murray, daughter of the Bishop of Rochester. Camden's builder was Augustine Greenland.

ST PANCRAS PARISH

St Pancras parish, to which Camden Town belonged, was an elongated one, stretching from Highgate Village to nearly Oxford Street, and east to west from York Way to Regent's Park. An early settlement stood near the old parish church in Pancras Road but from the 14th century the population decamped to Kentish Town, leaving the old church 'utterly forsaken'. The reason for this emigration was both an excess and a lack of water.

The excess came from the Fleet river. Two streams, one beginning in the Vale of Health at Hampstead, the other at Kenwood, met at Kentish Town and meandered down through today's King's Cross, Farringdon Road and Street, to Blackfriars, there to disgorge into the Thames. This picturesque feature, however, became a liability, for as London grew the lower reaches of the stream became polluted and clogged up. The Fleet, which was once navigable for sizeable boats up as far as today's Holborn Viaduct, became a sewer of unspeakable filth and stench, and in the upper reaches, especially at St Pancras where there was and still is, a low-lying plain beneath the old parish church on its knoll, floods resulted in rainy times. It was not for nothing that the area was often called Pancras Wash.

So, while the parish church remained on its old site, the parishioners despaired of its muddy and flooded vicinity and moved elsewhere. But they went to Kentish Town and not to the area of Camden Town. Here again the reason must have been water: Kentish Town had springs whereas Camden Town had too much clay to permit them. And, alas, even the pure but brackish Fleet running through the fields of lower Kentish Town was savoured only by cattle.

The parish was not the only local administration. There were manors also, medieval divisions with residual duties. These may be briefly summarised as Cantelowes manor, mostly owned by Camden on the east side of the High Street stretching up to Highgate Village, and Tottenhall manor, owned by Lord Southampton on its west. There was, too, the rump of Rugmere manor, one which had virtually disappeared when Henry VIII took a great chunk for his Marylebone Park. What was left lay north of Parkway and west of Chalk Farm Road, and was bought by Lord Southampton in 1786 and merged with his Tottenhall land.

The manors and their owners also added place names. Cantelowes, once owned by a prebend of St Paul's Cathedral, is commemorated as also is a prebendary, Thomas Randolph; Agar Grove (named from an irascible lawyer who lived at Elm Lodge in the vicinity) was once St Paul's Road. The Southampton family were not so methodical in this matter in Camden Town as they were further south, but

the family names of Arlington, Mornington and Fitzroy are sprinkled around.

Completion of Camden Town took a long time. Though Camden Road ('the New Road to Holloway and Tottenham') was constructed in the 1820s it was not until the 1850s that streets on either side of it were built. For some years the grander Camden Square area was called Camden New Town, no doubt an estate agent's ploy to disassociate it from the deteriorating social status of Camden Town itself. Meanwhile, Southampton completed streets south of Primrose Hill, his development complicated and sometimes spoilt by the advent of the London to Birmingham railway.

5. *Survey of the Borough of St Marylebone*, 1834, engraved by B.R. Davies. The parliamentary area of St Marylebone included St Pancras parish. Reproduced here is the Camden Town and Regent's Park portion, which shows the London & Birmingham Railway north of the Regent's Canal. By this time some of the streets on both sides of the High Street had been developed, and the burial ground for the parish of St Martin-in-the-Fields, off Camden Street, had been opened. Note also Elm Lodge, a large house to the east, whose owner, William Agar, had failed to prevent the Regent's Canal going through his grounds. The spur of the canal may be seen going down behind Clarence Street (Albany Street) and the barracks to terminate at the hay market.

6. *Camden Square*, *c*1905. The development of 'Camden New Town' along the Camden Road took place much later than the building of the original streets of Camden Town, and was of a much higher quality.

7. *Sydney House, Camden Square.*

8. *Camden Villas*. A pair of detached villas on Camden Road.

9. *No. 119 Camden Road* in *c*1960.

10. *Pastimes of Primrose Hill* by Isaac Cruikshank (1765–1811?).

ON PRIMROSE HILL

Fashion and social aspirations can determine an area's perceived boundaries. At times it has been important to be in or out of Kentish or Camden Towns; conversely, it has always been advantageous to be in Highgate so that even those halfway to Kentish Town have claimed it as their residence. Some prefer to be in Primrose Hill rather than Chalk Farm, but here confusion arises: where does one end and the other begin, or, more pertinently, are they one and the same thing? For that matter, where does either one of them become Camden Town?

Some topographical history is required here. Eton College acquired the Chalcots estate in 1449. This land stretched south-westwards from Haverstock Hill almost down to the line of Avenue Road, and north to south from England's Lane and Eton Avenue to, and including, the London landmark of Primrose Hill; it then ran along the back gardens north of today's Regent's Park Road to Chalk Farm Station. By the 17th century there were two farm houses associated with the estate, Upper and Lower Chalcots (a word which means 'cold hut' and has nothing to do with chalk). The first was on the Eton estate at the southern end of England's Lane in Hampstead, and the latter, just over the boundary in St Pancras, on the site of the present Chalk Farm Tavern.

So, strictly speaking, Chalk Farm (deriving from Chalcots) describes much of the Chalcot estate belonging to Eton College in the parish of Hampstead, and also that land adjoining the Chalk Farm Tavern, largely part of the old parish of St Pancras. Very confusing, but at least people in these two areas who identify with 'Chalk Farm' have a case. 'Primrose Hill', on the other hand, a name which can and does radiate in all directions, is a modern area designation and is used happily by many people in what is properly Chalk Farm.

11. *Primrose Hill and Chalk Farm* in 1836. A watercolour, artist unknown.

The actual Primrose Hill escaped development, but only just. Early schemes to cover it with houses in the 1820s, or to use it as a site for a botanical garden, came to nothing, and in 1829, a bizarre project was announced to burrow into the hill to form a vast cemetery which would take 5 million bodies. This plan was the brainchild of one, Thomas Willson, veteran of at least two grandiose but unbuilt mausoleums. He proposed that the cemetery should be in the shape of a pyramid, resting on a square about the size of Russell Square, and with a height beyond that of St Paul's. He proclaimed that his 'grand Mausoleum will go far towards the glory of London' and that 'every deposit' would be 'hermetically sealed for ever'.

Happily, nothing came of Willson's scheme, nor of a later plan to turn the area into a cemetery. The Crown Commissioners were persuaded to take over Primrose Hill for a public park in 1841, when it bought out the Eton College interest and about six acres from Lord Southampton. (Those six acres, which front Regent's Park Road, were called Rugmere field, a last vestige of the old medieval manor.)

As for the Chalk Farm Tavern, the first sight we have of this is possibly in 1678 when a Middlesex Justice of the Peace, called Edmund Berry Godfrey, was found murdered on Primrose Hill, impaled on his own sword. On discovery, Godfrey's body was taken to 'The White House', which has been identified by some as an early version of the Chalk Farm Tavern. The crime was a famous one and Primrose Hill achieved some notoriety, though it is probable that Godfrey was murdered elsewhere and his body merely dumped on the Hill. This was the era of Titus Oates and perjured allegations of Catholic plots to topple Charles II. Oates alleged that Godfrey was a victim of papists, and three, probably innocent, men were hanged after trumped-up evidence was heard. The key witness later withdrew his accusations, but by then the men were dead; the mystery was never solved.

The Tavern is noted again in 1803 when, after a duel on the Hill between Lt. Col. Montgomery and Capt. Macnamara, the former expired after being carried to the house. Macnamara escaped a manslaughter charge with the support of character references from Lords Hood and Nelson.

In 1699 the parish registers record the death of a 'stillborn vagrant' that lay in Chalcot barn and again, in 1703, the death of Susannah Jones, 'bastard child of a vagrant mother lying commonly in the Barn at Chalcott'. This barn was, no doubt, attached to the tavern.

The subsequent history of Chalk Farm Tavern is related on p93.

A PARK FOR DISCERNING PEOPLE

The creation of Regent's Park, most of which is outside the area of this book, did, however, affect the development of Camden Town. The Park's origins lay in the desire of Henry VIII to form a hunting park near to Whitehall, and in 1538 he had a roughly circular area, contained within the manors of Tyburn and Rugmere, surveyed. It was unwise to decline his offers of compensation and so Marylebone Park was established. The area taken did not conform to any particular topographical, manorial or historical features and so odd bits of land, such as the rump of Rugmere manor already referred to, were excluded.

A mound, later surmounted by a fence, ringed the Park. This kept the deer in and helped to keep the public out. Various lodges were built and as a hunting estate the Park continued until the Commonwealth period. Then it was put up for sale, advertised as having 534 acres, 124 deer, 16,297 trees – oak, ash, whitethorn and maple included – 2,805 of which were reserved for the Navy. Unfortunately, just as icons came down during this period, so did the trees, and by the time of the Restoration the character of the Park was entirely different. Afterwards came a pastoral period in which the virtually unwooded fields served as meadows.

It needed no genius to realise that the grid-like extension of the good-class estates south of the Marylebone Road, typified by Harley Street, could be carried northwards to the great benefit of the Crown's coffers. Fortunately for London the right people were there at the right time to prevent this – the Prince Regent as patron and John Nash as architect and designer.

Nash's scheme for the development of Regent's Park consisted of two circles, inner and outer, giving access to numerous villas and substantial palace-like terraces around the perimeter. His vision was only partially realised: eight villas were completed but two of the terraces were abandoned so that views of the northern heights were retained. Inside the park one feature was to affect Camden Town – the canal, and outside to the east of Albany Street on Crown land unused in the grand scheme, were created a barracks, and a market area to serve the new inhabitants.

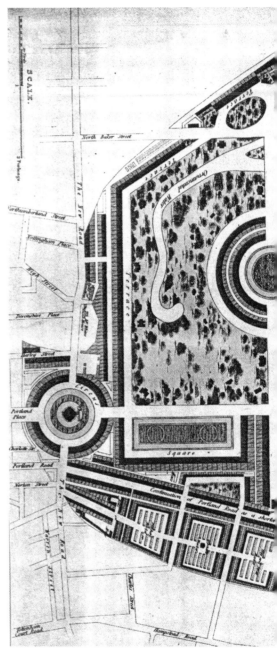

12. *Plan for Regent's Park.* Nash's original plan for the Park in 1811, with a double ring of terraces around the Inner Circle and the two crescents on the north. The proposed barracks were later built in Albany Street and the northern side of the Park was left open to keep the views of the northern heights.

ENTERTAINING THE EMPEROR

A very early resident of the Camden Town area was William Bruges, appointed in 1415 the first Garter King of Arms. He was responsible, as is his successor at the College of Arms today, for the registration and supervision of the grants of heraldic arms. Bruges features in the Cantelowes court rolls of the period; his landholdings are recorded but, tantalisingly, without hard evidence as to their precise location. He appears in state records as having entertained the Emperor Sigismund during his visit to this country in 1416. Bruges met the Emperor's procession, which had come from Ely Palace in Holborn, one mile south of Kentish Town – probably at today's King's Cross. The assembly was one of great magnificence. It consisted of the livery companies of London and the Lord Mayor and aldermen, the king's trumpeters, officers at arms, esquires and knights, the Bishop of Ely, the Dukes of Briga and Holland, the Prince of Hungary and other court luminaries. Bruges knelt bareheaded to receive them and then escorted them to his house for entertainment and feasting. Minstrels and sackbutts diverted them, and the food, which included nine pigs, seven sheep, one hundred pullets, one hundred pigeons, thirty capons and twenty hens, hares, rabbits, kids, salmon, eels, crabs, oysters, wild boars and red deer, satisfied their other wishes.

The Bruges house is thought to have been on the east side of St Pancras Way at today's junction with Agar Grove. It was moated, had its own chapel, possessed a 'great barn' and had a frontage of 130 yards on the 'London to Haringay' road. In the late 17th century its occupant was William Woodhouse, a local magistrate. In his journal (which is in the Camden Local Collection) he remarks that the house was 'a decayed mansion, more than half of which was uninhabitable, and used for barns and stables'. The house contained a 36-foot long hall on the ground floor, and there were various coats of arms in the house, including that of Bruges.

13. This view from the *Panorama of Kentish Town* by James King depicts the east side of Kentish Town Road, leading down to the Mother Red Cap. The range of houses were on the site of the rear of the present Sainsbury store and the Fleet river is roughly beneath the overhead railway track.

THE RIVER FLEET

The course of the river Fleet in Camden Town may be seen on the map on p10. But it is also visible in two views drawn by James Frederick King portraying the area as he recalled it, or thought it was, in about 1800. In the first view, illustration 13, the artist is standing at the southern end of Kentish Town Road looking south-east. Nowadays the horses would be approaching the rear of the Sainsbury store. The Fleet is near the centre of the picture, emerging from beneath the road and going towards St Pancras Way. A footpath coming from Kentish Town bridges it; this path is approximately the line of today's Royal College Street and the bridge was just south of today's Baynes Street. The river bisects Barn Field – the barn, belonging to dairy farmer William Francis, is in the distance. We cannot, unfortunately, see Mr Francis's farm house, which was in St Pancras Way facing today's Agar Grove, and nor does it feature in any other of King's drawings because that side of St Pancras Way was not drawn. This is a pity, because a view of the Francis farmhouse might have helped to solve the mystery, dear to the hearts of local historians, of the locations of Cantelowes 'manor house' and the first St Pancras workhouse, which was opened in 1731.

The location of that workhouse is discussed on p33. It is possible that it was situated in the old Cantelowes manor house. But then again the location of that manor house is far from certain. It could

have been on either side of St Pancras Way, in the area of today's Agar Grove. The manor house might also have been the same house in which William Bruges, the 1st Garter King of Arms, lived in the 15th century.

As far as the manor house is concerned, what are we to make of two field names on the parish map of *c*1800? An oblong field next to Mr Francis's house on the west side of St Pancras Way is called Bowling Green field, which indicates either a private luxury or a communal facility. Then again, on the other side of the road further north just before Kentish Town proper is reached there is a large space called Hall Field.

The manor house, in any case, did not shelter the lord of the manor since the lordship was vested in a prebendary of St Paul's Cathedral. Perhaps originally it was occupied by the steward of the manor and later by one of the more prosperous farmers. To add to the confusion, other writers have placed this house much further up the road, in Kentish Town, by Caversham Road.

Illustration 13 also shows the Mother Red Cap, still in its ancient form but with the almost compulsory 18th-century addition of tea gardens. Nowadays, of course, the Camden Road, built after this view, cuts away to the left of the pub.

14. *Mother Damnable, the remarkable shrew of Kentish Town,* the legendary original Mother Red Cap.

15. Another view from King's *Panorama*, this time the west side of Kentish Town Road. The site of the present Underground station is to the left, with stocks and pound in front of the parish workhouse. The Fleet river may be seen towards the right of the picture on a course which will take it behind the Castle Tavern which had tea-gardens on its banks.

A second view of the Fleet is given in King's drawing of the scene directly across the other side of Kentish Town Road. This stretch of road was often called Water Lane, which King tells us was due to the frequent flooding of the river as it ran beneath the road. This view is particularly interesting because it contains the only known illustration of the second St Pancras Workhouse on the site of the underground station. However, it is likely that King's drawing of the building is entirely inaccurate. The artist in his commentary beneath the drawing says that before being used for a workhouse it was a gentleman's mansion and then became the Mother Black Cap – his drawing demonstrates that it might well have been a mansion but gives no indication of a later use as a tavern. However, contemporary maps show that the ground plan of the workhouse was substantially different to Mr King's depiction; furthermore, a Vestry minute of 1802 notes that 'the construction is very slight, and the materials of which it is composed very indifferent, and now much decayed.' For those reasons we must suspect that Mr King, making his drawing much later, was guessing.

On the far left of the view is the fenced pound in which stray animals were kept – they were released by the parish officer on payment of a fine. Visible, too, are stocks just to the right of the pound, which were used for punishment of minor offences. The building numbered 1 housed a parish fire engine and a temporary lockup to hold prisoners before they could be arraigned in front of a magistrate. The building marked 5 is an oddity, described by Mr King as a 'soap manufactory' situated in the Hampstead Road. This stood on Camden High Street, just south of Hawley Crescent.

16. *Brown's Dairy Farm* beside the river Fleet. Brown's Dairy was eventually to be on the site of the Underground station, but the site of his farm is not known.

17. *Park Village East* by T.H. Shepherd.

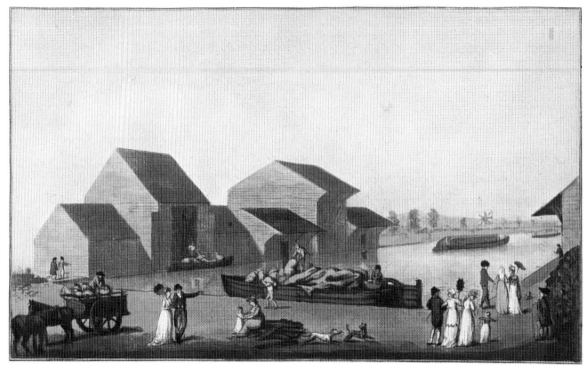

18. *A View of the Bason of the Grand Junction Canal at Paddington*, published in 1807.

The Regent's Canal

A LONDON CANAL

The opening of the Grand Junction Canal at Paddington in 1801 changed that rural area into a trading depot. Vast amounts of manufactured goods from the Midlands, destined for London or Europe, now had a bulk transport system which arrived at the Paddington Basin. Boats came down also loaded with vegetables, straw, hay and animals – the days of laborious cart journeys and the driving of herds for long distances were ending. But an even more lucrative prize was possible – a link from Paddington down to London docks, a scheme promoted by one, Thomas Homer. He reckoned, and probably with some justification, that not only would canal traffic increase anyway but that much of the tonnage at that time being shipped off the canal on to the Thames at Brentford could, in future, go straight to the docks in London's east end on his proposed 'London Canal'.

As it happened the proposal to connect the Paddington Basin with the docks coincided with John Nash designing Regent's Park. Not everyone regarded canals as decorative features, as we shall see later, but Nash was happy to incorporate it in his grand scheme. In 1811 he announced that the Prince Regent had approved the route of the canal through the new park and to it being named after him. The 'Regent's Canal' was a considerable coup for Homer and his associates and they pressed on quickly. Excavation began in October 1812 and by June 1814 work had advanced to the Camden Town area by a route which had so far met with little difficulty other than the removal of Mr Lord's cricket ground to its present site.

THE CUMBERLAND MARKET

At Camden Town a spur was constructed from the point where the canal goes beneath Prince Albert Road to just north of Robert Street off Hampstead Road. This route went between Park Village East and Park Village West, and behind the Albany Street barracks. Just south of the barracks was built the Cumberland Hay Market which replaced *the* haymarket south of Piccadilly Circus. In fact this was the most northerly of three markets planned, but the only one built – the others were meant to specialise in meat and vegetables. The Cumberland Market was not a success, despite its diversification into other commodities: it had a vast ice house be-

19. A view of the grounds of Elm Lodge, through which the Regent's Canal was built. This drawing, from James King's *Panorama of Kentish Town* depicts the house itself but it bears little resemblance to the Elm Lodge in illustration 20.

neath its main building where ice from Norway was stored. This was later filled in with rubble from the construction of the Piccadilly line extension to Cock-fosters.

A map of the mid–19th century shows wharves here dealing with coal and timber; in particular marble and stone were off-loaded intended for the clique of monumental masons that operated on the Euston Road (near today's Warren Street station). The market closed in 1926 and from that time the canal spur was filled in: its route is marked by the car park to the Zoo and may be further detected by looking over the wall at Gloucester Gate bridge at the rear gardens of Park Village.

TROUBLE WITH MR AGAR

The main course of the canal went off from Regent's Park into the virtually untouched fields of Camden Town on its way to Islington. It was on this stretch that the promoters had most difficulty. First, the experimental locks, which had been installed at Camden High Street, did not perform as well as promised and in the end conventional locks had to

replace them. Then, although the promoters had Parliamentary approval to dig the canal, they had not reckoned with the litigious William Agar, himself a lawyer, who had in 1810 built a house called Elm Lodge east of St Pancras Way and was disinclined to have his rural quietude disturbed by the splash of boats. In 1813 he discovered four or five men walking over his land surveying a route for the canal; he drove them off with violence and then resorted to law. He had his servants put up barriers to exclude the navvies in 1815, all the while driving up the compensation price. Matters were not finally resolved until 1832 even though the canal had actually opened as far as Islington by 1820; by then the tussle with Agar had cost the promoters a great deal of time and money. Nowadays, of course, a canal going past his garden would *increase* the value of his house, but Agar considered it differently.

A third, almost catastrophic development, was the discovery in 1815 that Thomas Homer, who had it seems no financial stake in his own brainchild (Nash had much of the equity), had been embezzling substantial sums of money, and had absconded abroad.

DAYS OF COMPETITION

Though the coming of the London to Birmingham railway signalled the long-term demise of the canal as a bulk carrier, the positioning of the rail goods yard west of Chalk Farm Road was actually, at first, a bonus for the waterway. After all, the railway had the same dilemma as the Grand Junction Canal: because its goods line went no further than the outskirts of London it still had to get much of its cargo down to the docks, or, particularly in the case of coal, in bulk to other areas of the metropolis. One local big user of coal was the Imperial Gas Works in Pancras Road, whose Victorian gasholders are so admired by conservationists today; these works had been built on the canal for the very reason that coal could be got to them in bulk on the water.

In the short term the canal was actually more a nuisance to the railways than the other way round. When the London & Birmingham Railway was extended to Euston it had to bridge the canal, and cope with an incline down to Euston so steep that at first trains, as we shall see, had to be hauled back up it by cable as far as the goods yard. The Great Northern had to tunnel beneath the canal to King's Cross and the Midland into St Pancras both tunnelled beneath and bridged over the water.

The Canal was never the profitable scheme dreamed of. It cost more to build than anticipated and the revenues were insufficient to pay off the debts and provide a good dividend. Increasing competition from the railways, especially from the Great Northern and Midland carrying coal and beer, meant that decline on the canal was inevitable, even though undramatic. Over a million tons was still transported in 1898 but this had slipped to nearly three-quarters of that by 1927.

EXPLOSION ON THE CANAL

The Regent's Canal was left increasingly with the inner London trade, such as carrying building materials and, sometimes, dangerous goods. The conveyance of gunpowder brought about a famous explosion on the canal in 1874. A steam-tug towing five barges set off in the early morning of 2 October from the City Road Basin, laden with grain, sugar, petroleum, and five tons of gunpowder destined for Nottingham. It was as the convoy got to Macclesfield Bridge – the one which connects to Avenue Road – that an explosion, still unexplained today, occurred. The noise was heard all over London and was thought to be an earthquake or the 'crack of doom' by some; severe damage was done to the area, not the least because the explosion also ripped open a gas main carried over the bridge. The keel of the gunpowder barge fell on a house three hundred yards away; in the Zoo birds escaped from damaged cages and the giraffes 'were found huddled together in terrible fear', with 'the monkeys trying to avoid the falling glass'. Such was the confusion that a posse of cavalry arrived from the Albany Street barracks under the impression that there had been a Fenian attack.

20. *Elm Lodge* in 1853.

21. *The Explosion on the Regent's Canal*. From the *Illustrated London News* 10 October 1874.

22. Preparing to 'leg it' through a tunnel on the Regent's Canal.

CAMDEN LOCK

The most obvious reminder today of the canal era in Camden Town is Camden Lock, now developed anew for leisure and shopping. There still stands the lock-keeper's house. His duties were numerous, including breaking ice in winter, toll collecting, inspecting the tonnage and, of course, supervising the opening and closing of the heavy lock gates. The ice on the canal, incidentally, was not a wasted asset. Mr Carlo Gatti, the well-known restaurateur and ice-cream maker, had a contract to collect the ice, which he stored in 60ft-deep wells by the canal at New Wharf Road, King's Cross. Ice breaking barges drawn by horses and rocked by a team of men did the initial work of smashing the ice. The canal ice was not, of course, particularly pure but Mr Gatti gradually organised himself to receive about a quarter of a million tons a year from Norway, which was better, and this was off-loaded at Limehouse and brought up to New Wharf Road.

Dingwall's wharf on the basin at Camden Lock was the works of T.E. Dingwall, a packing-case manufacturer, who moved here in 1937 from the City Road Basin. The attraction of the site was, of course, that timber could be shipped here in bulk from the docks. On the other side of the basin once stood a petroleum depot where barges, or 'tar tanks' as they were known, off-loaded petroleum.

What is known as the 'interchange' warehouse stands nearby, now renovated and ready for office use. As can be seen from the towpath it was possible to bring barges right into this building, there to connect with the railway goods depot which occupied the warehouse. On the other side of the canal is Gilbey House, designed in 1937 by Chermayeff as the head office of Gilbey's, the wine merchants; barrels were lifted off barges from projecting galleries.

The canal could not have functioned without horses. These great shires, led along the towpath, pulled the barges and, where a tunnel prevented this, the horses were disconnected and men lay on their backs on a platform on the barge and with their legs on the walls of the tunnel, propelled the boat through. This was very hard work, but in the long Islington tunnel the canal proprietors brought into service a fiery steam barge which pulled each boat through. Two ramps – horseslips – are situated on each side of the railway bridge at Camden Town so that horses which fell into the canal could be led to a place where they could get out.

Pickford's, who had a depot at City Road, were by far the largest carriers, and the fastest. They employed 'fly-boats', pulled at a trot by pairs of horses in relays, covering the usual four day trip to Birmingham in two and a half days. The firm later moved their centre of operations to Camden Town, but this was to be next to the Camden Town goods yard of the railway.

A MODERN CANAL

The canal's future as a recreational asset was signalled just as real decline had set in. In 1951 John James, who has been closely associated with the modern canal, began operating his painted narrowboat, *Jason*, from Little Venice, up and down, introducing new generations to this hidden part of London. British Waterways introduced river buses, the *Jenny Wren* began operations from Camden Town, and the towpath was at last opened up to a curious and appreciative public.

The most astonishing change has come at Camden Lock, where what began as a modest market with one or two bars and a restaurant and dance hall, has become a thriving tourist attraction. Its metamorphosis is described on p140.

23. At Camden Lock in the early 1970s, when the Dingwall business was still in operation. The 'Interchange' warehouse is in the background.

The Workhouses

WITCHCRAFT MANIA

Near the end of the reign of Elizabeth I the great Poor Law Act of 1601 placed the responsibility for relieving the poor squarely on the shoulders of the parish. It was accepted that the old haphazard system of parish pensions and private charity could not make up for the alms and shelter previously given by monasteries suppressed by Queen Elizabeth's father. Furthermore, there was a greater mobility of people, especially of the poor, seeking employment in other parishes and particularly in London.

The St Pancras Vestry minutes of 1730, which record that certain members were empowered to 'look out in the Parish for a Propper and convenient house for a workhouse to Lodge and Imploy the poor of the said parish, and to agree for the rent thereof' has always been taken to indicate the first workhouse in the parish.

But in a journal (already mentioned on p19) kept by a local magistrate, William Woodhouse, at the beginning of the 18th century it is implied that an earlier workhouse existed locally. It is mentioned in a story concerned with the murder of an old woman, believed to be a witch.

Woodhouse reports that in 1703 an old man living at the Castle Tavern, at the southern entrance of Kentish Town, announced that he and his wife had been bewitched by an old couple who lived in a cottage in the fields. It 'was cried out in all the neighbouring parishes that they were to be tried by ducking on such a day, when, about noon, a great concourse of people to the number of 1000 appeared in the town.' It should be said that the punishment of ducking into a pond or stream, the person usually strapped to the end of a plank, was one normally inflicted on women, such as 'scolds' or alleged witches. Mr Woodhouse continues: 'The officers of the parish had privately removed the poor old couple in the dead time of the night to the church, as a place of safety. The mob demanded these unhappy wretches *at the workhouse*, on being acquainted that they were not there, they pulled down the pales and walls, broke all the windows, and demolished a part of the house. After searching the chimnies and ceilings without effect they siezed [*sic*] the governor, hauled him down to the stream, and declared

24. *Workhouse Kentish Town*. A view of the workhouse opened by the St Pancras Vestry in 1731. The artist is looking south-east towards St Pancras Church; on the right the man is fishing in the river Fleet.

workhouse Kentish Town

25. In this view taken from King's *Panorama of Kentish Town* the artist depicts the 'Ruins of Old St Pancras Workhouse in 1790 transferred to a plot of Ground the corner of the Hampstead Road & the Kentish Town Road.' King, drawing this in 1848 either from memory (he himself was born in 1781) or from someone else's recollection, puts the workhouse on the east side of St Pancras Way, near to the junction with Agar Grove. This contradicts illustration 24. The ruins could possibly have been the last vestiges of the medieval house of William Bruges, first Garter King of Arms.

they would drown him and fire the whole village, unless they delivered these poor creatures into their hands.'

The poor couple were found in the vestry room of the chapel and dragged to the stream, presumably the Fleet, and 'after much ducking and ill-usage the poor old woman was thrown quite naked on the bank, almost choaked with mud and expired in a few minutes, being kicked and beat with sticks even after she was dead, and the poor man lied long dangerously ill from the treatment he received. To add to their barbarity, they put the dead witch (as they called her) in bed with her husband and tied them together. The master of the workhouse, fearing the consequences to himself, it was who informed these wretches where these two poor old people were secreted.'

It is difficult to know where this appalling event took place, since Mr Woodhouse has the couple hiding first in the church, implying Old St Pancras Church, and then in the vestry room of the 'chapel' which could only mean Kentish Town Chapel. The location of the workhouse is also unknown.

A NEW WORKHOUSE

The whereabouts of the St Pancras Workhouse opened in 1731 is not clear. We know from Rocque's map of *c*1746 (see illust. 1) that it was in St Pancras Way, about where Agar Grove now joins that road. But the words on his map could apply to houses on either side of the road. Illustration 24 shows the workhouse to the east of the river Fleet and, presumably, St Pancras Way running in front of it to the left of the picture; St Pancras Church is seen in the south-east. This would indicate that the workhouse was on the *west* of St Pancras Way. However, King's drawing shown in Illustration 25, has the ruins of the workhouse on the *east* side of the road.

In 1772 the building, wherever it was, was declared unsafe but it was not until 1775 that the parish officials met to consider the adaptation of a 'house called Mother Black Caps, or the Half Way House', and another three years before inmates moved in. This building was, as we have seen, on the site of Camden Town underground station. But by 1787 the wards were so overcrowded there that five and six persons slept in one bed, and there was a dread of putrid fever breaking out. The rooms were small, the windows inadequate and the timbers decayed. In 1809 it was reported: 'On examining the bedsteads, the number is 224, 52 of which are single and 97 double bedsteads, all of which may be fit for use if they be cleansed from vermin.' The remaining 75 were stated to be useless.

This description is included in a report that year on moving the effects of the Camden Town workhouse to the new building on Pancras Road, just north of the church.

26. The Royal Veterinary College. The usual dating for this watercolour is 1805. However, the large building in the background poses a problem. Though the perspective is not quite right the only building that was on the other side of St Pancras Way and to the north-east of the College was Elm Lodge, which was not built until after 1810. It will be seen also that the house as depicted here is entirely different to the two versions in illustrations 19 and 20.

The Royal Veterinary College

The map of St Pancras parish of *c*1800 shows the Veterinary College, its grounds backing on to St Pancras Way (thereby including part of the Fleet river) and extending to paddocks on the other side of what became Royal College Street.

Oddly, for a country which relied so heavily on animals, especially horses, England was backward in veterinary science. What treatment there was for injured or sick animals was given by jumped-up far-riers, sometimes called horse-doctors.

The first veterinary college in Europe was estab-lished in 1762 in Lyons and was used as a model in other countries, but not in England. Not until the beginning of 1791 did a committee of interested men, chaired by Granville Penn, grandson of Wil-liam Penn, set in motion a scheme for a college in England. As their first principal they appointed a M. Vial de St Bel, from the Lyons establishment,

who was principally interested in horses and their anatomy and who became well-known for supervis-ing a seemingly ill-judged post-mortem on the famous racehorse of the time, Eclipse.

The College was established at a general meeting on 8 April, 1791 and by September was actively looking for premises. M. St Bel urged the committee not to choose a marshy or low ground, because of the putrid vapours exhaled, to choose a site which was reasonably near to the metropolis but far enough away to avoid temptation to the students.

The choice of Camden Town appears to have been a chance one – it could just as well have been anywhere in the rural fields around London where there was a water supply. The land at Royal College Street seems to have been offered them in response to a newspaper advertisement placed by the com-mittee. Lord Camden's offer is minuted as being 'for about 100 acres of building land...abutting on the Turnpike Road leading to Kentish Town which is intended to be called Camden Town...' This is an ambiguous minute in the Veterinary College re-cords, because the 100 acres applied to much of Camden's estate rather than the two acres or so that

the College initially took. The site included a house, which fronted St Pancras Way, that was to be the home of M. St Bel. The agents for the transaction noted to the committee: 'We will only add this land is on an eminence with plenty of fall for water with a small Rivulet running through the same...' Those familiar with the area will know that the College is not built on an eminence and, indeed, was in just the area where the Fleet frequently flooded in flash-storms.

In September the matter was settled and James Burton, architect and developer, was instructed to prepare plans for the College buildings, and the following year a further four acres were taken across the road for a paddock. Despite a desperate shortage of money the scheme proceeded and while building work was in progress M. St Bel, a touchy man of limited knowledge and ability, who had declined to return to France because of the Revolution, taught the few pupils that there were in his house. The College was almost immediately engulfed in an internal dispute when the qualifications of St Bel were called into question. He managed to gain a vote of confidence but he died the following year.

The first horse was admitted for treatment here on 1 January 1793. By this time there were fourteen pupils.

St Bel was succeeded by an autocrat called Edward Coleman and it was to be this man who managed the College for nearly forty-six years and who guided its development in both physical and tutorial terms.

A memoir by a former student, who was at the College in 1828, gives us an idea of the buildings of that period. He notes that 'the Institution was built in a Quadrangle Form, having now in the centre a large lawn or grass plot surrounded by posts and chains, and that between the Buildings and these a broad Pathway had been left, partly paved with stones...used chiefly for testing the freedom from lameness of Horses. In the central part of the Lawn, a Mound, planted with trees and shrubs, concealed from view a large Water-tank, protected by a strong iron grating. From this source the water – needed by the whole Institution – is drawn, the supply to the tank being furnished by the New River Company.' He goes on to describe the paddocks and stables. Noting the house which Coleman had taken over

27. *M. Vial St Bel demonstrating to a shoeing-smith* in front of the Veterinary College building. 'Ignorance' is disappearing to the left.

28. Activities at the Veterinary College. Sketches published in the *Illustrated Sporting and Dramatic News*, January 1888.

29. Examining an injured horse on the floor of the covered courtyard.

from St Bel, he said that 'Being situated on the opposite side of the Fleet, it was approached from the College buildings by a strongly-built Rustic-bridge which spanned the river just in front of the Forge at the north end of the Ride. It may here also be explained that after the main source of the Fleet was diverted, the portion of it which originally formed the boundary of the site granted for the building of the College, became a stagnant Ditch which in process of time dried up, and that, with the addition of gravel and earth, a dry path from the College to the Professor's house was thus constructed'. The garden was 'not only protected originally on the College side by the Fleet Ditch, but by a Thorn-planted Hedge, which extended onwards to the Bridge in Fig Lane (Crowndale Road) thus also enclosing the 'Green' at the back of the Elephant & Castle Inn'. The inn referred to stood on the site of Goldington Court and was, of course, the College local. It was kept, during this student's time, by a Mr Wrench who made sure the students were not excessive: he 'will never allow more than a proper quantity of either ale, wine or spirits...'

Various buildings were tacked on over the years but in November 1937 the present buildings, which entirely replaced the old structure, were opened by George VI; the architect was Major H.P. Maule.

The location of the College here may have been a chance but, as it happened, it was a fortuitous one. During the most prosperous railway age the College was near to two of the largest users of horses in London – the goods yards at Camden Town and at King's Cross. Gradually, the expertise of the College covered many other species – the letter from the Regent Pet Stores (see illustration 128) shows that they were dealing with monkeys. In the archives of the College at Royal College Street is a letter, dated July 1935, which, however, shows the experts to be at rather a loss:

'Dear Sir,
Will you kindly let me know which is the surest and most humane way to destroy a tortoise?

The reply, after some delay, read:
So far as I am aware, the members of the College staff have never been asked to destroy a tortoise here, but I should think that the most humane way would be by shooting.'

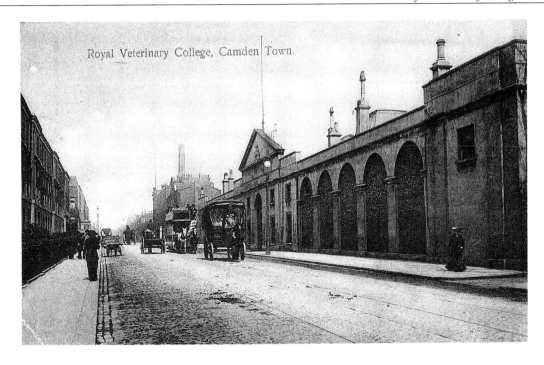

30. *The Royal Veterinary College* and Royal College Street, *c*1905.

31. Rear view of the Royal Veterinary College.

32. *The Zoological Gardens*, an engraving by T.H. Shepherd.

Wild Animals in the Park

More exotic kinds of animals were being studied on the other side of Camden Town. The Zoological Society of London began, it seems, as a proposal by Sir Stamford Raffles, founder and governor of Singapore, for a 'zoological collection which should interest and amuse the public.' This resulted in the Society's formation in February 1826: Raffles, who was appointed chairman, died the same year.

The committee was dissatisfied with the site (the present one) offered them in the Park. It was felt that the situation was too public and restricted and that the area later taken by the Royal Botanic Society was preferred. In correspondence with the Commissioners of Woods and Forests, who managed Regent's Park, it was pointed out that the plan 'would be to have a garden laid out in aviaries, paddocks for Deer, Antelopes, etc, stabluaries for such animals as may require them…and if possible pieces of water for fish and aquatic birds. Our buildings would for the most part be low and in no case offen-

sive'. This plan 'should not only make an establishment attractive in itself but extremely ornamental to the Regent's Park'.

Decimus Burton laid out the first gardens and designed their buildings. As befitted one who had built some of the villas in the Park his Zoo buildings were small follies, with elegance placed before animals. Over the years, other fine buildings were added. The popular lion house of 1876 was designed by Anthony Salvin jnr. Many readers will recall this building and the cramped conditions of the animals but it was a great improvement on the previous house. In 1869 a magazine said: 'Lions at play, free as their own jungles at home; tigers crouching, springing, gambolling, with as little restraint as on the hot plains of their native India – such is the dream of everyone interested in Zoology. We are all tired of the dismal menagerie cages. The cramped walk, the weary restless movement of the head…the bored look, the artificial habits… Thousands upon thousands will be gratified to learn that a method of displaying lions and tigers, in what may be called by comparison, a state of nature, is seriously contemplated at last'.

Such has been the movement of public opinion that the even more liberating lion terraces which superseded Salvin's admired buildings are now

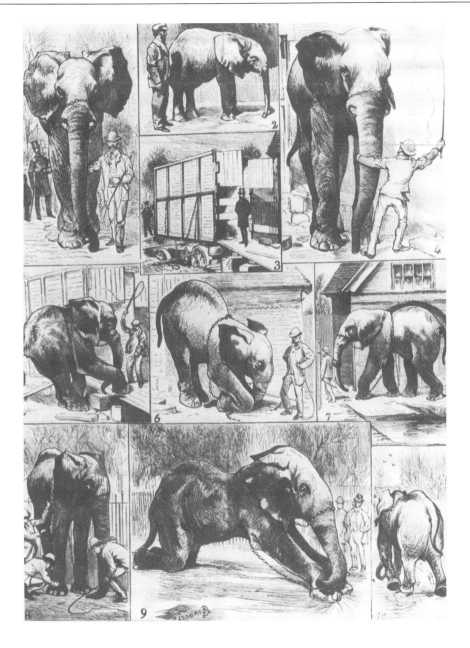

33. The Jumbo saga. The elephant, Jumbo, had been a principal exhibit at the Zoo since 1865. In 1882, it was agreed to sell him for £2,000 to Barnum's Circus in the United States. But the elephant refused to leave and his persistent reluctance caught the imagination of press and public. The press said that Jumbo was being separated from his long-term mate, but an official history of the Zoo points out that this was untrue, and in any case Jumbo was proving to be, in his old age, a dangerous animal and might at any time have to be put down. The Zoological Society reasoned that rather than having a dead animal they could get a good price from Barnum instead. The author does not comment on whether the Zoo should have sold a dangerous animal to a circus. Eventually, Jumbo was persuaded to leave and he ended his days in America.

34. One of the classic Underground posters of the
between-the-wars era.

considered inadequate and oppressive. And scarce-
ly anyone could not have been moved by the pro-
found boredom in the gaze of the large gorillas.

In any rearrangement of the Zoo, if there is to be
one, account must be taken of several buildings
which are considered to be architectural classics.
The Mappin Terraces, for example, designed by J.J.
Joass with Sir Peter Chalmers Mitchell, were
opened in 1914, reminiscent of a feature in Ham-
burg Zoo, but much criticised as a habitat for the
animals. The Berthold Lubetkin penguin pool of
1934 is thought, by some, to be a piece of sculpture
in its own right. The Elephant and Rhino Pavilion of
1965, by Sir Hugh Casson and Neville Condor,
architecturally announces the animals it houses, but
one cannot help but feel dispirited at seeing the
space limitations within it.

The Zoo's public side overshadows its research
activities, and, to an unusual extent, this learned
society is linked in the public mind with the adequa-
cy or not of its buildings. Probably no other institution has such a record of building replacement and
improvement and yet attracted so much criticism for
their form.

At the time of writing the future of the Zoo is in
doubt. A cash crisis threatens its survival as a
straightforward Zoo and there is much talk of
alternative schemes to show the work of the Society
in the conservation of species. Many would like to
see the Zoo continue but the novelty of encounter-
ing animals face to face has diminished as television
has showed them in their natural habitat, and the
rising cost of entrance deters many parents. The
dilemma for the Zoo is that those animals most restricted by the site area, and which many think
should not be in this kind of captivity, are the very
ones that appeal to the public at the turnstiles.

Rails Through Camden Town

THE LONDON & BIRMINGHAM RAILWAY

No part of London kept its social aspirations intact after close encounter with the new railways. That mechanical invasion leaves its blighted areas today: King's Cross is a byword for derelict property and the neglect of successive administrations; the Waterloo area is dilapidated; and whole swathes of Kentish Town, hiding railway sidings and interchange facilities, are only recently being renovated. In Camden and elsewhere the tracks indelibly separate communities.

The London & Birmingham Railway (from 1846 called the London & North Western) arrived in Camden Town at a crucial time. Not only did it delay development on the Chalcots estate, with Adelaide Road as a main avenue, but it also predated and therefore affected the building of much of Chalk Farm.

The new-fangled method of transport came understated. In 1830 the incipient railway company claimed: 'The railway will either pass under or over the great roads, never on the same level, will be carefully fenced everywhere and ornamental when in sight of gentlemen's residences; the carriages make little noise, the engines produce no smoke.'

There were certainly cynics around who feared if not the worse, then an unpleasant change, but noone could have imagined the impact the railways were eventually to have. Thomas Rhodes, who farmed the fields of the Chalcot Estate (and indeed those opposite Mornington Crescent), spoke for many at the time the railway company was promoting its Bill in Parliament:

'The measure [for making a railroad] is viewed by most of the landholders as fraught with bad consequences to their interest, and the Middlesex farmers who have already suffered so much by the Canal consider this Rail-Road as likely to produce their utter ruin. It is hardly possible to let a Farm in Middlesex *now* but upon the most deteriorated terms. I hope the College will not only withhold their consent but contribute their powerful aid to the opposition which is making to the Bill and that it will ultimately be thrown out.' Others thought that

35. *Construction of the London & Birmingham Railway* (1836), by J.C. Bourne. The cutting shown here is just south of the Parkway bridge.

36. *North View of the Camden Station of the North Western Railway.* This drawing must surely have inspired the author of the *Thomas the Tank Engine* books! To the left is the Roundhouse.

LONDON AND BIRMINGHAM RAILWAY.

HOURS OF DEPARTURE,

Commencing 4th June, 1838.

	FROM LONDON.	FROM DEN. HALL. *By Coach to Rugby.*	FROM RUGBY.	
DOWN	7½ A.M.	10 A.M.	2½ P.M.	to BIRMINGHAM
	9½ A.M.	12	4½ P.M.	to do.
	*11 A.M.	—	—	to DENBIGH HALL.
	1 P.M.	3½ P.M.	8 P.M.	to BIRMINGHAM.
	* 3 P.M.	—	—	to DENBIGH HALL
	* 5 P.M.	—	—	to do.
	7 P.M.	—	—	to do.
	8½ P.M.	—	—	to do. (*Mail*)

	FROM BIRMINGH⁰	FROM RUGBY. *By Coach to Den. Hall.*	FROM DEN. HALL.	
UP	—	—	4 A.M.	to LONDON. (*Mail*)
	—	—	*7 A.M.	to do.
	—	—	*9½ A.M.	to do.
	—	—	*1 P.M.	to do.
	—	—	*5 P.M.	to do.
	9 A.M.	10½ A.M.	3 P.M.	to do.
	12 A.M.	1½ P.M.	6 P.M.	to do.
	1½ P.M.	3 P.M.	7½ P.M.	to do.

ON SUNDAYS.

	FROM LONDON.	FROM DEN. HALL. *By Coach to Rugby.*	FROM RUGBY.	
DOWN	7½ A.M.	10 A.M.	2½ P.M.	to BIRMINGHAM.
	*9½ A.M.	—	—	to DENBIGH HALL.
	*5 P.M.	—	—	to do.
	8½ P.M.	—	—	to do. (*Mail*)

	FROM BIRMINGH⁰	FROM RUGBY. *By Coach to Den. Hall.*	FROM DEN. HALL.	
UP	—	—	4 A.M.	to LONDON. (*Mail*)
	—	—	*7½ A.M.	to do.
	—	—	*5 P.M.	to do.
	1½ P.M.	3 P.M.	7½ P.M.	to do.

The Mail Trains do *not* stop at any Station between London and Denbigh Hall.
The Trains marked (*) stop for Passengers, at *all* the Stations.
The remaining Trains *only* at Watford, Tring, Leighton, Denbigh Hall,
Rugby, and Coventry.

37. Timetable of the London & Birmingham Railway in 1838.

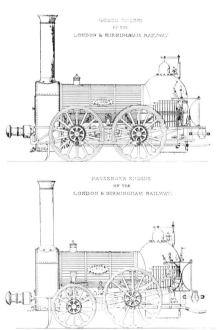

38. Goods and passenger engines on the London & Birmingham Railway, from Wishaw's *Railways of Great Britain and Ireland*.

39. *The Station at Euston Square* (1837), by T.T. Bury. This interior view of the first Euston Station gives a good idea of the nature and *size* of carriages of the time.

the smoke of the passing engines would seriously discolour the wool of their sheep.

Rhodes, incidentally, farmed land which made up much of the site of Euston Station, and an engineer of the London & Birmingham has recorded that Rhodes endeavoured to maintain on it a thousand cows, but that, 'do what he would, he could never exceed 999'.

The opposition of Eton College, and that of Lord Southampton, who had been a resolute opponent in the Lords, was bought off by money. In the case of Eton the bargain included a tunnel beneath their estate for much of the route through it, and a tunnel, what is more, sufficiently strengthened to support buildings on top.

The Primrose Hill tunnel became a tourist attraction. Visitors from afar gazed with wonder at the engineering, the formidable architecture, and the ominous power of the locomotives as they emerged from its darkness.

It was planned originally that the terminus should be at Chalk Farm with the line finishing just north of the Regent's Canal – this intention, either achieved or projected, is shown on an 1834 map of the area. But it became obvious soon that a more central London site for a terminus was necessary, and Euston Square was chosen. It was this 1835 afterthought that was to complicate matters because the canal had to be crossed, either under or over. The latter method was chosen, resulting in a steepish gradient south of the canal, too sharp for the locomotives of the day and, indeed, difficult for years afterwards. A large winding engine was therefore erected in the goods yard near the south of today's Gloucester Avenue, to power a cable that hauled engines up from Euston. This necessitated the construction of two tall chimneys to take away the smoke of the furnaces powering the engine. These stacks were in themselves a tourist attraction and a pub in the Chalk Farm Road advertised a view of them.

40. *Camden Town Fixed Engine Station,* from Simms' *Public Works of Great Britain.* These two towers were a landmark at Chalk Farm and even a tourist attraction in their own right.

In 1837 the daily service consisted of three trains with as many as forty small carriages in each. This dearth of traffic and the diminutive size of the trains must be remembered in considering the nature of the building in Chalk Farm that began at about this time. The iron road was not then the omnipresent and smoky leviathan it became. Indeed, it must have seemed rather quaint and jolly.

The presence of the railway may be anticipated now as one walks from the grander buildings of Regent's Park Road and Chalcot Square, down to Gloucester Avenue, although the declining status of buildings may also be put down to the distance away from Primrose Hill. However, the standard of houses in Gloucester Avenue is very much better than in many streets in London, built next to railway lines. The 1834 map of the area shows no Gloucester Avenue at all; an 1849 survey has villa-type residences at the southern end of the road, and it is reasonable to assume that these grander houses, designed by Henry Bassett and shamefully destroyed in recent years, were built or planned before the extension of the railway from Chalk Farm to Euston had progressed. Putting those villas aside, the later houses on the railway side of that road are fairly substantial. It may be noted here that the extension of the railway to Euston resulted in a realignment of the proposed Gloucester Avenue, hence the sharp curve as the canal bridge is crossed.

It is pertinent to compare what must have seemed almost a pleasantly rural era that had the occasional rumble of a train, to what is was like in the 1950s in Gloucester Avenue. This author, whose first London lodgings were in this road, remembers the whole street bathed in smoke for much of the day; indoors was the grime of the corrosive dust that spread from the sidings and main line.

At the time Gloucester Avenue was being built the trains were uncoupled from their engines at Chalk Farm and rolled down by gravity, with men riding as brakemen, to Euston. The journey back was accomplished by men pushing the train up to a bridge just outside Euston and then connecting it to the cable which hauled it back up to Chalk Farm. This system remained until 1844.

The transfer of the passenger terminal to Euston opened up the land at Chalk Farm entirely for train maintenance and goods handling. A long, oblong train shed was built beside Gloucester Avenue – to be the bane of residents' lives eventually, as the trains frequently just stood there emitting smoke. The goods engines were maintained in the Roundhouse and gradually firms like Pickford's transferred their handling facilities from the canal to this yard.

The London & Birmingham, or LNWR as it became, was essentially a long-distance line. The first stop out of London was Harrow and so it could not

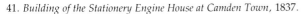

41. *Building of the Stationery Engine House at Camden Town*, 1837.

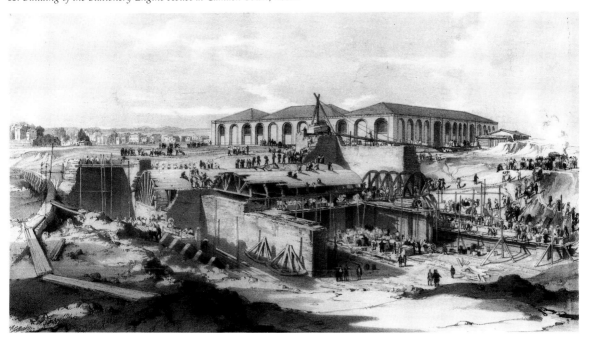

42. *Camden Town Engine Sheds*, *c*1935, by Norman Wilkinson. An evocative LMS poster (The LNWR w
merged into the LMS in 1923).

have encouraged building development in Camden Town. But the construction of the line brought low-paid, usually Irish, workers to the area and it is from this era that Camden Town's Irish population derives.

There is no doubt that the intensity of railway activity in Camden Town led to a deterioration of streets around. Within recent memory the condition of the buildings on both sides of the track was the saddest in the area; it was these houses which were let out, vastly overcrowded, to poorer people looking for accommodation near to their employment, quite often on the railway itself. Electrification has changed much of that and encouraged people to take gambles on restoring houses close to the line.

In addition the LNWR put into quarantine a whole area of Camden Town to the west of Chalk Farm Road which is even now mostly hidden behind a high wall. We must hope that this, like the grime, will disappear soon.

The railway line, as it was enlarged, and as the trains got bigger and the traffic increased, made an impact in Camden Town. One side of Park Village East was lost and houses on Hampstead Road demolished. Mornington Crescent, which was built before the extension to Euston was considered, had its views of and relationship with Regent's Park rudely shattered.

THE ROUNDHOUSE AND CAMDEN GOODS YARD

A major building of that railway construction age remains in Camden Town – the Roundhouse. It was designed by Robert Benson Dockray, engineer to Robert Stephenson, who lived in Pancras Vale, a stretch of road now absorbed by Chalk Farm Road. Although the Roundhouse was an ingenious building it was quickly outdated. In it the early engines were serviced; the engine would enter from the west and would then ride on to a turntable in the centre of the building which could then transfer it to any of the twenty three inspection bays around the perimeter of the building. The Roundhouse became useless when the size of the engines was increased and they would not fit onto the turntable or into the bays. Beneath the bays were inspection pits and underneath the whole was a warren of tunnels.

In fact, the bulk of the Goods Yard (always called after Camden it should be noted, although the site was not on his land) was honeycombed with tunnels. The purpose of most of these appears to have been the transfer of horses from one task to another without crossing rails: stables existed for the poor creatures in the vaults beneath the Roundhouse and elsewhere.

43. *Goods Forwarded by Railway*. A part of the Pickford's depot at Camden Town.

44. Scenes from the various premises of Gilbey's, the wine and spirits company, at Camden Goods Yard.

The carriers, Pickford's, were a substantial element in the Goods Yard. But the name which came to dominate the area was the wine importers and distillers, Gilbey's. The company had been formed in 1857 by Walter and Alfred Gilbey, who had served in the Crimean War as clerks in the Army Pay Department. The original trade was in wines only, but in 1887 they bought a distillery in the Glenlivet area in Scotland. By 1914 the firm occupied twenty acres at Camden and every day a whole train, known as the 'Gilbey Special', left for the London docks. Gilbey's also occupied the Roundhouse and it was probably they who built the wooden gallery; other buildings were occupied by them near the canal and by Oval Road. In 1879 the hours of work at Gilbey's publicised during an industrial dispute, were long: they were Mon-Thurs 7.45am–6.30pm, Fri. 7.45am–7pm, and Saturday 7.45am–2pm. These were later reduced and the rates of pay increased to 30 shillings per week for the better class of worker and 21 shillings for the lower class.

AN ABORTIVE SCHEME

A rare map of 1838 reveals a plan to build another line, the London Grand Junction Railway, from the Camden Goods Yard to the London Docks. As will be seen in illustration 45, this would have had a dramatic effect on Camden Town. It is not clear from the plan if the proposed line went over or under the canal, but either way it would have meant disaster, for it would have been at bedroom level just like the North London, or it would have been constructed in a cutting right through the area.

What this map also shows is that a western side of Mornington Terrace was never built – in fact the eastern side was not constructed until after the extension of the London & Birmingham to Euston was built.

A FORGOTTEN RAILWAY STATION

The Midland Railway came last into our area and had to take what route was left to it. Its construction resulted in the notorious excavation of the old burial ground at St Pancras, work which was partly supervised by the young Thomas Hardy. The line from St Pancras went over the canal, under the North London Railway and Camden Road, and cut through the streets east of Kentish Town Road to the railway station there. On its way it spawned a station at the corner of Sandall Road and Camden Road, the site of which is now a petrol station. Hardly any evidence of it is left, but the fact of the railway beneath the road there is the reason for the two petrol stations – no substantial buildings could be put above it.

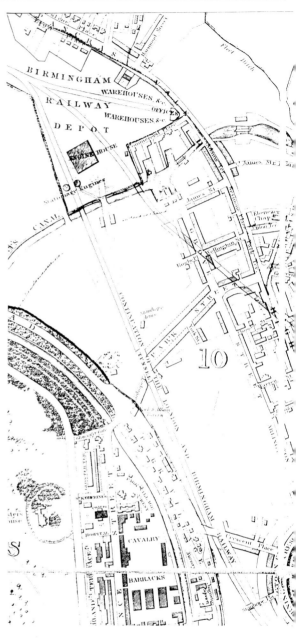

45. A map dated 1838, which appears to be an amended version of the map shown in illustration 5, shows a proposed railway line from Camden Goods Yard across Camden Town down to the docks.

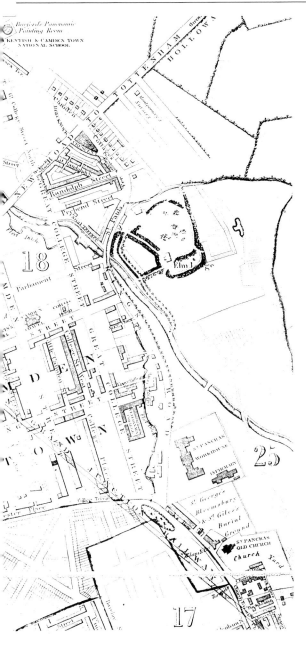

THE NORTH LONDON LINE

The North London Line, previously called the East and West India Docks & Birmingham Junction Railway, opened as far as Camden Town in 1850. It did not, as elsewhere, have a disastrous effect on the neighbourhood, although some areas, notably the little triangle near Baynes Street, and those just north of the underground station have it at bedroom level. The line at that time included a station at Primrose Hill which is, today, under threat of closure.

At first the line was popularly called the 'Camden Town Railway'. A long report in the *Illustrated London News* describes a journey in 1851 from Blackwall. Nearing our area he goes on: 'Through the high level of Islington the railway is in a cutting averaging 16ft deep with walls of massive brickwork. We quit this cutting near the Caledonian road, and cross the same by a bridge...We next passed over the Great Northern Railway; and it was a curious sight to see a monster Northern train, sixty feet below us, entering the tunnel running under the extensive tract of land known as Copenhagen fields. This is indeed one of the most singular views through which the railway passes.

'After passing several beautiful villas we arrived at Camden Town, where the railway is constructed on a brick viaduct of good proportions. We soon enter upon ground intersected with the rails of the Great North-Western Railway until we reach the end of our journey at the Hampstead Road [Primrose Hill].'

46. *Accident on the North London Railway.* On 16 August 1864 the explosion of a boiler caused a passenger train engine to plunge over the viaduct at Camden Road Station, landing in a yard behind Randolph Street. The fireman was killed and the driver injured. Fortunately, the carriages were not pulled over.

The Early Shopkeepers

An area's standing is reflected in its shopkeepers. Those listed for Camden Town by 1805 catered for the most basic needs: they included a truss maker as well. But on the whole they were generally a mix of grocer, butcher, smith and shoemaker, the sort of thing any decent village would have.

Camden High Street did not have that name. It was fragmented, as developers tried to inject some exclusivity into the block they were building, into terraces. Camden Place stretched from the Red Cap down to Pratt Street, south of that was Pratt Place; around the corner in Fig Lane (Crowndale Road) was Gloucester Place. On the other side of the road Pleasant Row (again indicative of a developer's selling methods) went south from Park Street (Parkway); halfway to Delancey Street it became Warren Place. South of that was Delancey Place and Southampton Row.

By 1809 there was a wider spread of merchandise, but the shops were by no means concentrated. An analysis of the traders and private residences shows them to be spread up and down the High Street, with residential properties between, and round the corner into Crowndale Road.

The early Camden Town traders listed below are taken from an 1809 London directory.

CAMDEN PLACE
(Mother Red Cap to Pratt Street)
John Anderson, flour factor
P. Felix, pattenmaker
A. Lucas, haberdasher
John Westbrook, shoemaker
Joseph Earley, plumber and painter
Mrs Ireland, boarding school

PRATT PLACE
(Pratt Street to Crowndale Road)
John Balm, wax and tallow chandler
John Cummins, builder
J.S. White, engraver
William Bundy, comb manufacturer
G. Hodd, victualler
Joseph Salisbury, baker

PLEASANT ROW
(Parkway to Underhill Street)
Anne Dixon, butcher
Robert Graham, nurseryman
Charles Mathews, grocer
Edward Moore, baker
Samuel Wallis, baker
Robert Wells, ale and table beer maker

WARREN PLACE
(From Underhill Street to Delancey Street)
Samuel Banks, surgeon

DELANCEY PLACE
(From Delancey Street to Mary Terrace)
Holmes, artist

47. *The Britannia Hotel.* A Britannia pub existed in Camden High Street, at the junction with what became Parkway, as early as 1777 – before the development of the area. This engraving of probably mid–19th century shows a rebuilt hotel of some elegance.

Pianos in Camden Town

The manufacture of pianos was centred in Camden and Kentish Towns. This was a development of the specialisation in furniture and upholstery traditionally associated with the Tottenham Court Road area, the only remnant of which is today exemplified by Heal's furniture shop. The new industry would have also taken advantage of the adjacent canal for the bulk transportation of timber.

The advent of the pianoforte was signalled in an advertisement for its performance at Covent Garden in 1767. The instrument was popularised by John Christian Bach (the 'English Bach' as he was called), who was buried in St Pancras churchyard in 1782. But Camden's connection with the piano begins with a musician called Muzio Clementi, the first genuine composer for the instrument. By 1809 he was in partnership with a man called Collard in the Tottenham Court Road and by 1831 Collard & Collard were leading manufacturers for the booming trade in pianos. It was their circular building which still stands today in Oval Road. This is a 22-sided brick structure of the mid-nineteenth century with five floors, previously with a central hoist, which superseded a similarly shaped building destroyed, a year after it had been built, in 1851.

John Brinsmead had a factory in Grafton Road but also, from 1923, his company was in Royal College Street. Brinsmead had the rare distinction of celebrating seventy years of marriage – both he and his wife were 92 at the time. Salter & Son, a breakaway from Broadwood's, another famous firm, worked from 98 Camden Road both as music publishers and pianoforte manufacturers. Their early advertisements claimed that their pianos were 'warranted to stand in Hot Climates, at the lowest possible prices consistent with good workmanship'.

The 1892 Directory, commonplace in this respect, records numerous businesses around Camden Town associated with pianos. Some are quite small, working from houses, with small specialisations like covering the piano hammers; others, such as one in Bayham Street, made keys; but there are many well-known names in the business, with full-blown factories, such as Challen & Co in Arlington Road, and Monington & Weston in King's Yard. The old Challen factory in Pratt Street, next to the St Martin's Tavern, still survives.

48. Advertisement for Salter & Son, piano manufacturers and music publishers of Camden Road. From an 1892 Directory.

Charles Booth in his *Life and Labour of People of London* (1903) recorded that a standard working week in the piano industry was between 54 and 56 hours in winter and 48 in summer.

An old piano factory still stands at 44 Fitzroy Road after a sustained campaign to prevent its demolition. This was the works of John and James Hopkinson, built in 1867. It is now converted into flats.

Less well known was the industry making mechanical pianos – called pianolas today. Clementi and Collard devised one in the 1820s and, more recently, they were being made by Pesaresi and Son and Spinelli in Early Mews. In Royal College Street John Arrigoni made barrel pianos and also street organs. Organs proper were made in the Rotunda Organ Works, a circular building just north of Wilmot Place, now the site of St Richard of Chichester School. This was the factory of one of the most famous of organ builders – Henry Willis. The building had originally been used for painting panoramic views, such as those painted by Horner in his long days strapped to the dome of St Paul's Cathedral.

Places of Shelter

THE ALMSHOUSES

One step up from the workhouse was an alms-house, although this could vary widely in its provisions and accommodation. Camden Town contained two groups.

The first, which still survive, were the almshouses belonging to the parish of St Martin's in the Fields, Westminster, opened in 1817, overlooking an extra-mural burial ground for that overcrowded parish, opened when Camden Town itself was uncrowded. The aim of the almshouses was to provide accommodation for seventy widows and unmarried women, who were also given about £2 a month and medical care. A writer, commenting in 1874, is critical of the arrangements: 'Each poor old lady has but one small room, which evidently serves the purpose of sitting-room, bed-room and kitchen' and goes on to suggest that the St Martin's authorities could well visit the St Pancras Almshouses and come away with ideas that 'might lead to improvements being made in accordance with the sanitary and social advancement of the present day...'

The burial ground itself, once called Camden Town Cemetery, was consecrated in 1805. Not only was it used for those buried from St Martin's parish from that date, but it was also to take the remains of much older burials when the churchyard of St Martin-in-the-Fields was being cleared. This has led to claims, difficult to deny or sustain, that people like Nell Gwynn, originally interred in St Martin's churchyard, ended up in Camden Town.

An attempt in 1855 to build on part of the ground in which interments had taken place, aroused local opposition and riots. The St Pancras Medical Officer of Health reported in suitably grisly terms of the coffins and skeletons being disturbed, the risk of disease and so on. There was also then a strongly-held conviction that the remains of the dead should be left in peace.

In the face of such criticism building works were delayed but the matter was not resolved until 1887 when St Pancras Vestry agreed to take over the burial ground; in 1889 it was opened by the Countess of Rosebery as a public garden. At the same time a handsome Greek cross, erected by public subscription and a local music society, marked the grave of local resident Charles Dibdin, the composer of many sea-songs including *Tom Bowling*.

49. *The Boys' Home, Regent's Park Road, c1905.*

The actual grave is now very vandalised and dilapidated. Dibdin was an ancestor of the Conservative politician, Michael Heseltine, one of whose names is Dibdin.

Buried here was also Dr George Swiney, a relative of the chemist, Sir Humphrey Davy, who bequeathed a large sum of money to endow a Lectureship.

Another set of almshouses existed in the little road called Rousden Street, off Camden Road. These were founded in 1840 by Mrs Esther Greenwood (they were originally named after her), a niece of the actor, Joseph Munden; she herself lived in Cumberland Terrace, Regent's Park. A marble tablet was erected, in what is now the Greek church in Camden Street, to the effect that the almshouses were intended to 'provide an asylum, rent free, for aged women of indigent circumstances and good character – a preference being given to the inhabitants of Camden Town and Kentish Town.' The women, who had to be over sixty years old, had two rooms each.

These almshouses were on the north side of the road and have since been replaced by houses, apparently built in the 1930s.

50. *Bow Cottage*, a building in the courtyard behind the Boys' Home, which was used by them.

THE REGENT'S PARK BOYS' HOME

The Home for the Maintenance by their own Labour of Destitute Boys not Convicted of Crime was begun in 1858 at No. 44 Euston Road by a Mr W.G. Bell, who was distressed at the number of beggar boys on the streets. Among the earlier supporters of this venture were Frederick Denison Maurice, founder of the Working Men's College, and Thomas Hughes, author of the famous book *Tom Brown's Schooldays*.

In 1865, when the Midland Railway came to the Euston Road, the Home was displaced to Regent's Park Road, at the corner with King Henry's Road; four years later about a hundred boys were sheltered there. Their routine was the usual hard one of the time. They rose at 5.45am, had drill at 6.15am, then cleaned the premises, had breakfast at 7.45, followed by prayers and work until lunch at 12.30pm. There were lessons in the afternoon, wood-chopping at 5pm, prayers and play afterwards, and bed at 8.30pm.

This was not an unusual diet but their food, consisting of more than just the bread, gruel and occasional meat to be found in many homes, had additional delicacies like rhubarb pie and treacle pudding. When a boy left he received a suit of clothes and some money.

The Home was closed in 1920, but much of the actual building survives.

51. The Bakery in the Boys' Home.

ARLINGTON HOUSE

The enormous hostel for men in Arlington Road, now called Arlington House, was one of several in London built by Rowton Houses Ltd, a public company which stemmed from philanthropic work begun by Lord Rowton in 1892. Arlington House was the last of the hostels erected by the Company; it was designed by H.B. Measures and opened in 1905. It was also the largest, with 985 cubicles and 118 'bedrooms', meaning, in this context, rooms which were large enough to regard as private sitting rooms with space for more possessions than the usual overnight things. The exterior design is governed by the original internal provision of 7' x 5' cubicles, each with its own window, so that the design is one of many small windows at regular intervals.

Rowton's venture was begun in a different era. There was no dole, no social safety net; the lodging houses which existed for single men were vastly overcrowded and had poor sanitation. Rowton's innovation was to provide private cubicles instead of dormitories, and his ideas were copied in many towns here and abroad. The later image of these hostels was not the one which existed at the time.'The men strive to maintain their position by coming in to our houses and take a pride in living in them and it is our duty to make it as desirable a residence for them as possible.' There spoke a Victorian, but as time went on these ideals became diluted. Also the premises got older and harder to maintain, and the prospering world outside became more hostile, not only to the men, but to the continued appearance of a poverty which was thought to have disappeared under the welfare state.

Rowton Houses, being a limited company and not a charity, were able to dispose of their 'hostel' function. For example, Camden Town's counterpart at Mount Pleasant became a hotel and is now being rebuilt as a Holiday Inn. At Camden Town conditions deteriorated. The staff, who were generally recruited from the residents on quite low wages, took industrial action against the conditions for both themselves and the inmates. Old-style disciplinary rules still existed, summed up in a 'punishment book' for the early 1980s, in which inmates are fined, usually £7, for wetting their beds or other misdemeanours.

Rowton Houses wanted to be out of the hostel business and Camden and the GLC took on the responsibility. Since Camden took over the funding (management is by a separate trust) Arlington House has improved dramatically and now, at a time of extraordinary homelessness, it is a credit to the borough and to those, such as the Arlington Action Group, who further its interests.

Matters of Sanitation

A PUBLIC BATHS

The first public baths in Camden Town were in Plender Street, between Bayham Place and Camden Street on a piece of ground that had escaped development – the pub, the Parr's Head, is on the same piece of ground, just west of the site of the old baths. The freehold of the land was purchased but there were, immediately, squabbles on the Vestry on the matter of the cost of the new venture. The Vestry was urged that the only way to economise was to reduce the size of the establishment, but it was pointed out that this would negate the whole purpose of the exercise and, incidentally, create a higher working subsidy per user.

The baths, which included two swimming pools each measuring 49' x 23', were opened in 1868. The row which had begun over the building costs had simmered throughout the contract and was to erupt in a petulant manner after the opening day when a complaint was made at the Vestry that 59 bottles of wine had been drunk at the inaugural ceremony.

But the public liked the building. Forty-nine weeks after the opening the Vestry was told that over 145,000 people had used the baths, and now there were large numbers using the washhouses as well. Local women came to do the family washing and staying, it was noted, an average of 3½ hours there washing, mangling, drying and ironing, and spending an average of 5½d.

These baths were demolished when the present housing development was built; appropriately, a laundrette stands on part of the site.

More exotically, a Turkish Baths opened at 11a Kentish Town Road, just north of today's Camden Town underground station, in 1878: it ceased trading c1910.

LAVATORIES FOR LADIES

Sanitary reform also included the provision of public lavatories. While there were plenty of urinals for men the provision of public conveniences for women was regarded as one of much delicacy. A Vestry committee in 1874 was told that several doctors had testified that the lack of lavatory accommodation for women had often resulted in fatal consequences. In 1875 a public company approached the Vestry with a view to establishing conveniences for women, which would include 'retiring rooms' for ladies and a free convenience for poor women and children. This plan came to nothing and in 1878 the Vestry were urged by the Ladies' Sanitary Association to do something in the matter. It was not until 1880 that a new plan emerged. A Mr Alfred Watkyns (of Paris!) applied to the Vestry for leave to erect public conveniences for both sexes. They were styled 'chalets de toilette et de nécessité'; 20' long, 12' wide and 10' high, they were made of iron and wood and wood-panelled to 6'; above that they were to have glass panels which contained, like modern bus shelters, illuminated advertisements. It was proposed to provide four water closets at each end of a chalet and to use a portion of each building as a 'kiosque' for the sale of newspapers and also to station a shoe-black at each end of the chalet. The company proposed to begin with an experimental chalet in Parkway, facing the intersection with Gloucester Avenue.

This was very French indeed and this, no doubt, inspired a protest from local residents who claimed that if the chalet were a 'pecuniary success' it would 'have a tendency to diminish that innate sense of modesty so much admired in our countrywomen'.

The saga was to continue. It was not until 1883 that the French chalet providers obtained the Vestry's permission to erect one at the junction of the High Street and Parkway.

52. *The Camden Turkish Baths* 1878. The premises, designed by H.H. Bridgman, were at 11a Kentish Town Road, just north of today's Underground station.

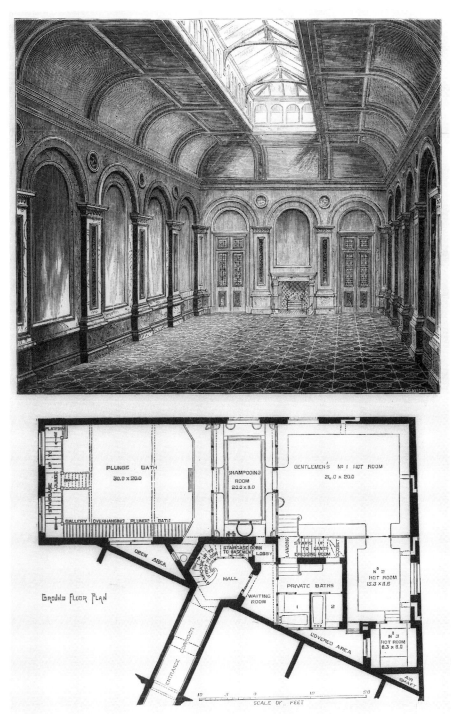

THE CAMDEN TURKISH BATHS.——Mr. H. H. Bridgman, Architect.

53. *The New Church, Camden Town* 1828, by T.H. Shepherd.
St Stephen's church, at the junction of Pratt and Camden Streets, was built in 1824 by the Inwoods.

Pulpits in Camden Town

ST STEPHEN'S CHURCH

The first churches in Camden Town were both built in 1824. One was for the Church of England, Camden Chapel, and the other for the Wesleyans.

Camden Chapel was built at the junction of Camden and Pratt Streets in 1824. It had probably been intended that Camden Street should become the principal avenue of Lord Camden's development, but if so it was an unrealised plan. It must be assumed, on the evidence of maps and ratebooks, that the building boom fondly hoped for did not happen. We must also assume that either Camden was too mean or too cautious to spend money on an Anglican church to attract early buyers, or else an initial and convincing lack of interest in the area led to a substantial delay in providing one. An 1874 writer commented that many speculative builders bought land for building purposes in Camden Town at the beginning of the century and a great many were unable to finish what they had begun. This failure of the initial scheme is underlined by the grander, and much later, development around Camden Square which was christened 'Camden New Town' in an attempt to attract a better class of occupant.

Camden Chapel was the work of William and Henry Inwood, father and son, who had recently completed the splendid St Pancras New Church on Euston Road. The architectural critic of the *Literary Chronicle* gave it a mixed reception.'On the whole,' he said, 'we consider it highly creditable to the taste of the architects, and an acquisition to the architectural beauties of the metropolis.' But, he went on: 'When viewed at a distance its general form is not particularly pleasing. The tower does not harmonize well with the body of the structure. The building is most advantageously seen at a short distance from the portico, where all the beautiful details and execution of the front are conspicuous.'

The architecture, as the critic told us, was derived from the Greek, and so it is particularly fitting that this church, which later was called St Stephen's and even later, All Saints, has served the Greek community since 1948.

The first minister at the church was the son of the writer, Madame D'Arblay. Attendances were good until the 1870s; in a census of church attendance in 1854 it was found that the average number of worshippers on a Sunday morning was 1650, in the afternoon 630 and in the evening 1430.

THE WESLEYANS

The Wesleyans built a chapel, also in 1824, in what was called Little King Street, now King's Terrace, behind the present Methodist chapel in Plender Street. In 1860, having outgrown these premises, they opened a new chapel at the south-east end of Camden Street. Meanwhile, the Primitive Methodists had held their first services in Camden Town on a patch of green in the area of Royal College Street and were later housed in Greenland Road, in a house previously used as a paint shop. About 1855 they moved to a room over some stables in Stucley Place and they also preached on Gospel Oak Fields. When the Wesleyans moved out of their chapel in King's Terrace the Primitive Methodists bought it for £275 and rebuilt it; they, too, outgrew the building, and in 1890 opened what was called the New Camden Chapel in Plender Street, today's Camden Town Methodist Church.

THE MORMONS

An 1849 newspaper cutting reports on a new phenomenon – the Mormons.'This sect is rapidly increasing in numbers in the neighbourhood of Camden and Somers Towns and intend in the spring of the year to emigrate and colonise in California. They have arranged to hire the use of four or five vessels for their own conveyance to the Western World. On their arrival in California, they intend to pursue their route to the 'Valley of the Salt-water Lake', enter upon farms, and encourage agriculture. They 'hold' all things common among themselves, and are strictly bound by the ties of fraternisation and socialism.'

The descendants of these adventurous people have in recent years been micro-filming the records and archives of both Camden and Somers Town so that any ancestors may be identified and retrospectively admitted into the Mormon faith.

THE EBENEZER CHAPEL

A fire and brimstone chapel opened in Kentish Town Road, just north of the underground station, in 1835. This derived from the activities of a Thomas Gittens, an upholsterer in the High Street, who had been engaged to fit up the pulpit and communion table for Camden Chapel. While doing so, and carried away as people are when left alone in a pulpit, he decided to become a preacher himself. He first broadcast his own brand of Christianity above a carpenter's shop in Bayham Street when the regular preacher failed to appear one Sunday.

PARK CHAPEL

The Congregational Park Chapel was opened in 1843 on the west side of Arlington Road at its junction with Delancey Street. Like many buildings of the period, it was destroyed by fire in June 1848, the result it seems, of carelessness by workmen repairing the ventilation. It was rebuilt from the insurance money and completed by November the same year. There are now flats on the site.

AGAR TOWN

Agar Town was a squalid settlement of jerry-built houses on the east side of St Pancras Way, north of St Pancras Old Church. Drainage and sanitation were of a minimum, and most of the overcrowded dwellings were no more than simple structures built straight on to the earth. Called Agar Town, because the land had been owned formerly by the William Agar who had been the bane of the Regent's Canal proprietors (see p27), it had become one of the most notorious slums in the country. Though it was outside the area of this book, its destruction, when the Midland Railway to St Pancras was constructed, brought about the erection of a new church in Camden Town.

A Report in 1847 stated that about five thousand people lived in Agar Town; there was no school, church or chapel in the entire neighbourhood, other than the Old St Pancras Church which, about this time was closed and being 'restored' from its medieval form into the pleasant Victorian building it now is. A temporary iron church was therefore erected in Agar Town, together with a Ragged School. Building of a permanent church began in 1859, under the supervision of S.S. Teulon, but it was never completed because the the Midland Railway, needing space for its goods yard, successfully sought its demolition. The Agar Town church, named St Thomas, was eventually located in 1863 in Wrotham Road, off Agar Grove, on land now part of a Council estate.

54. *St Thomas's Church, Wrotham Road, c1905*. This building is now demolished.

A NEW PARISH CHURCH

St Michael's in Camden Road superseded, eventually, All Saints in Pratt Street, as the parish church. It is on a very cramped site, and now overwhelmed by traffic, noise and, in particular, the aggressive Sainsbury building, but it has an interesting interior. One of its most ardent fans was Francis Bumpus who wrote in 1907, that 'St Michael's evinces an austere reserve of ornament, a scholarly and refined proportion, and a delicate and fastidious taste in colour that stamp it as one of the most beautiful churches built, not in London alone, but in England since the Reformation'. High praise indeed.

St Michael's was begun in 1880 – the tower originally proposed and depicted in the illustration was never built; consecration of the completed building did not take place until 1894, although it was in use by 1881. The architect was Thomas Garner of Bodley & Garner.

The present state of the church, particularly of the interior, gives much cause for alarm. The congregation here is very small indeed, one quite insufficient to meet the costs of the major repairs necessary.

NEW CHURCHES FOR NEW AREAS

Construction of Camden Road – the 'Road to Holloway and Tottenham' – began in the 1820s and development on both sides, which included Rochester
and Camden Squares, took place. This time on the
Camden estate, no mistake was made. The houses
were grander, the clientele was up-market and a
church was built – in fact the church was commenced in 1847 with the roads laid out but hardly a
house near it.

The consecration date, l849, is not without signifi-
cance, because it was this year that the old parish of
St Pancras, growing rapidly in population, was di-
vided into sixteen districts for ecclesiastical purposes.

St Paul's was by the architects Ordish and Johnson. Unfortunately, it was badly damaged in the
last war and eventually pulled down; it has been
replaced by an uninspiring successor.

The 1849 map also shows the temporary church of
St Mark's, Regent's Park. This was in the same position as St Paul's, Camden Square – there, but with
few neighbours. It had been opened in 1848 on the
site of 36 Regent's Park Road, probably on land don-
ated by Thomas Little, who was to be the architect
of the permanent church built nearby, consecrated
in 1853. Like St Paul's, St Mark's also was badly
bombed in the last war, but its fabric survived and
the building was reopened in 1958.

The Presbyterians had two churches in Camden
Town. Trinity Presbyterian Church was at the junction of Buck Street and Kentish Town Road; this
was rebuilt in 1909 and is now the Trinity United

55. *St Michael's Church, Camden Town*. The proposed
design published in 1881, but the tower was never built.

56. A view of St Mark's Church, from the bridge into
Regent's Park, *c*1905.

ST. MARK'S CHURCH, REGENTS PARK.

57. *St Paul's Church, Camden Square, c1905.*

58. *Our Lady of Hal* in Arlington Road.

Reformed Church, a joining together of Presbyterians and Congregationalists. The other was opened in Camden Park Road in 1869. Since the last war this building has been used for commercial storage and exhibition stand manufacture, but it has recently been entirely renovated, inside and out, and will survive, no doubt, well into the next century. It lost part of its tower at some time, and it has now gained some ugly aerial-type attachments.

The Baptists had Avenue Chapel, a small building overshadowed by the Idris factory in Royal College Street; this disappeared with the industrialisation of that area early this century. But in Chalk Farm the Baptist Church in Berkley Road has been there since 1871 (it was reconstructed after bomb damage in the last war).

Oddly, for an area so Irish, a Catholic church came late and it came by a circuitous route. A Belgian religious order, of Scheute, made itself responsible for the large number of Belgians who fled to London during the 1st World War and settled here. The Order was permitted to erect, soon after the war, a temporary church on the east side of Arlington Road, on the site of today's church hall, and in 1933 a permanent building, called Our Lady of Hal (Hal is a place west of Brussels in which there is a notable shrine to the Virgin Mary) was opened. About twelve years ago the Order relinquished its administration of this church and the building is now part of the Catholic diocesan system.

There had been an earlier organised Catholic presence in the large mansion, called Park House, at the junction of Gloucester Avenue and Gloucester Gate. This building had been bought about 1880 by an order of Catholic nuns, the Helpers of the Holy Souls, who had arrived from France in 1873. Park House was rebuilt in 1908–10 as Holy Rood House and has in recent years been a short-lived Japanese school.

Places of Learning

WELLINGTON HOUSE

Camden Town has contained three well-known educational establishments. The earliest was Wellington House Academy, which the young Dickens attended, the second was the North London Collegiate School for Ladies, Miss Buss's famous pioneering school for the education of girls, and the Working Men's College which, happily, still flourishes.

The Dickens family came to live in Camden Town in 1822, in some disarray and distress. They took on what was then 16 Bayham Street, a house identified as being on the site of today's no. 141, part of the hospital building. When Dickens recalled the house to his biographer, John Forster, he described it in the most critical way and he was hardly more complimentary about the area. He was, obviously, very miserable there. But, he was only ten at the time, he had been dragged out of school which he loved at Chatham, his father was in serious financial trouble, and in this tiny house of two storeys and a basement with, in effect, two rooms on each floor, were crammed his parents, five children, a servant, and a lodger. Dickens himself occupied a tiny garret room at the back, overlooking the backs of the High Street houses.

When Forster's biography appeared a contemporary of Dickens who had lived in Bayham Street at the same time, fifty years previously, leapt to the defence of the street. It was, he said, like a village there. Grass struggled through the newly-paved road. There were between twenty and thirty newly-erected houses. Residents included Mr Lever, the builder of the houses, a Mr Engelhart a celebrated engraver, a Captain Blake, a retired linen draper, the correspondent himself, a retired merchant, a retired hairdresser and a Regent Street jeweller. These were hardly people who would put up with squalor.

There seems no doubt that Dickens saw this street through the privations he endured in this period. One biographer, at least, has identified this house (or, at least, Dickens's recollection of it) as being the home of the Cratchits in *A Christmas Carol*. Dickens's father was sent to Marshalsea Prison for debt, on the complaint of a baker called James Karr of Camden High Street and young Dickens was sent to the famous blacking house at Charing Cross to work at a menial job. There must then have seemed little hope for him, deprived of social status and even of education.

In 1824, while the rest of his family resided at the prison with his father, the young Charles was

59. *Charles Dickens* when aged 18.

60. *No. 141 Bayham Street* (now demolished), the home of the young Charles Dickens in 1822. He occupied a tiny garret room at the back.

61. *Wellington House Academy* in Hampstead Road, which Charles Dickens attended.

lodged with a Mrs Roylance in the northern part of today's College Place. Gradually, the family fortunes improved and they moved to a house at what was then 29 Johnson Street off Eversholt Street – this is today's Cranleigh Street.

And then, to his relief, the family could afford to send him back to school. This was the Wellington House Academy, which stood at 247 Hampstead Road just south of Mornington Crescent. It was a conventional private school – one large room with several classes going on at the same time. Dickens wrote in 1849 that the railway had 'taken the playground, sliced the schoolroom, and pared off the corner of the house'. There was enough of the house left for Sickert to use it for both painting and teaching. A plaque was put on it in 1924 but the house was demolished altogether in 1964 when the railway bridge was rebuilt.

OLD WOMAN'S SCHOOL, CAMDEN TOWN.

62. *A Dame School in Camden Town*, location unknown.

63. *View of the Camden Town Infant and Sunday Schools*. These were built next to St Stephen's Church in Camden Street; the architect was T.M. Nelson.

EDUCATION FOR GIRLS

Education had hardly moved on by the time Frances Buss established her North London Collegiate School for Ladies on 4 April, 1850 at No. 46 Camden Street. She chose the location because of the number of 'Professional men' in the neighbourhood. On the opening day thirty-five pupils assembled, daughters of 'retired gentlemen, surgeons, artists, clerks and the most respectable tradesmen', all present at a momentous innovation in education.

Frances Buss came of an artistic family. Her father, Robert William Buss, had exhibited at the Royal Academy and had also done some etchings for the first edition of Charles Dickens' *Pickwick Papers* in 1836. Her mother was a strong believer in education for girls, and sent the young Frances to a small school, just like Dickens, in the Hampstead Road, where she later became an assistant teacher.

Her mother, in fact, had set up a small school herself in 1845, in Clarence Way, Kentish Town, where she taught pupils by the Pestalozzi method. Frances was a teacher here taking 'a select number of Young Ladies as Morning Pupils'.

The first college for women was founded in 1848 – this was Queen's College in Harley Street. Early enthusiasts for this venture included Frederick Denison Maurice (whom we shall encounter later in connection with the Working Men's College) and the Rev. David Laing, renowned for his campaigning zeal from his church in Kentish Town quite near to Mrs Buss's school. Queen's College was a teacher training college and Frances Mary Buss was one of the earliest pupils – another was Dorothea Beale, a lifelong friend and later the Principal of the Cheltenham Ladies' College.

The Buss school in Kentish Town flourished. But what Frances Buss wanted was a school for the girls of those middle-class families too poor to afford governesses and select academies. In many ways these girls were worse educated (because it was regarded as unnecessary) than poorer girls who quite often received some instruction at charity schools. With the active support of Laing and the Vicar of St Pancras she opened her school, when aged twenty-three, in her own residence in Camden Street. By December 1850, there were 115 pupils crowded into it.

Nowhere in any of the School's histories is the existence of a North London Collegiate School for Boys noted. This was established by St Pancras Vestry in January 1850, the same year that Miss Buss opened her school – again the Vicar of St Pancras and the Rev. David Laing were leading proponents. At the formation meeting it was resolved 'That regard being had to the wants of this populous and increasing locality, it is in the opinion of this meet-

64. *Frances Mary Buss* (1827–94).

65. *No. 46 (later renumbered 12) Camden Street*, the first home of the North London Collegiate School for Ladies. The house is now demolished.

66. Girls looking rather ill on the 'Giant Stride' in the gymnasium at Sandall Road.

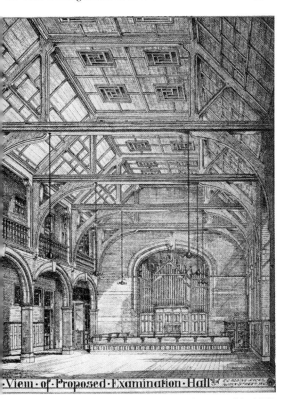

·View·of·Proposed·Examination·Hall·

67. *The Clothworkers' Hall* in Sandall Road, opened in 1879.

ing expedient that a public school be established in which a thoroughly sound commercial and classical education based on religious principles, can be afforded on economical terms.' This new school (which gets a mention in an 1874 history of the area – but the more important school of Miss Buss doesn't!) was at the bottom of Camden High Street, near the Camden Theatre site. It seems likely, bearing in mind the similarity of school names, the identical formation year, and the involvement in both of two of Miss Buss's closest supporters, that there was to be some kind of relationship between the two ventures.

Her family helped Miss Buss out. Her father taught art and science, two of her brothers taught Latin and Arithmetic; Laing instructed in scripture and Denison was always helpful.

During the next twenty years the school flourished – as did the reputation of Frances Buss. She and Dorothea Beale were formidable influences in the drive to secure education for women. When London University was persuaded to grant degrees to women in 1878, a pupil of the North London Collegiate was among the first women to obtain a B.A. Then, confident of the school's future, Miss Buss transformed her school, by means of a trust, from a private to a public institution.

Inevitably the school outgrew the address. While the North London Collegiate moved to new premises at 202 Camden Road Miss Buss opened another school in 1871 for younger girls at the old Camden Street address – this was called the Camden School. The Camden School outgrew, once again, the Camden Street house, and moved to Prince of Wales Road to the old home of the Governesses' Institution of which the Rev. Laing had been a strong and energetic supporter – the building is still there, now occupied by part of St Richard of Chichester School. In 1879, the first purpose-built school for the North London was built in Camden Road by Sandall Road, with generous help from the Brewers' and Clothworkers' Companies.

Again, space became a problem, especially playing space. The North London bought the magnificent old house Canons, at Edgware, for its playing fields and just as the 2nd World War began the whole school moved out of both their Camden addresses to the new building. It was as well, for in 1940 the Sandall Road building was gutted by bombing. After the war Sandall Road was rebuilt and the Camden School for Girls returned, leaving the higher school at Canons.

During this post war period some adjacent land that the Camden School had its eye on for development was taken by the Jewish Free School. The latter derived from a German Jewish school founded in Spitalfields in 1817. It had remained in the East End until the last war, but in 1958 opened its new building in Camden Road.

68. A cautionary notice relating to the North London Collegiate School for Boys, 1857.

69. *The Working Men's College*, Crowndale Road.

CAUTION

J. OSBORN was this day **COMMITTED TO PR** by the Magistrate at Clerkenwell, for Throwing S and knocking off the Caps of the Pupils of the N London Collegiate School :

And all Boys causing annoyance, are h Cautioned that the Magistrate is determined to with the utmost severity of the law, the next Of brought before him.

March 27th, 185

THE WORKING MEN'S COLLEGE

The famous Working Men's College began in humble circumstances in 1854, the brainchild of the energetic Frederick Denison Maurice. It first gathered in a house in Red Lion Square where a hundred and fifty workmen went to evening classes and learnt by gas light. Pressed for space it soon moved to Great Ormond Street, but in 1905 the building in Crowndale Road was opened, very near where Denison had helped Miss Buss over fifty years before to establish her innovatory school.

This new home, which had thirty classrooms, laboratories, gymnasium and music room, attracted teachers of great calibre and social awareness. They included Ford Madox Brown, Dante Rossetti, Ruskin and Lowes Dickinson.

70. *The Coffee Room, Working Men's College.*

71. *The Ruskin Art Room, Working Men's College.*

72. *The North London School of Drawing and Modelling* in Camden High Street, as depicted in the *Illustrated London News* in 1852. The School was founded in Euston Road in 1850. In the picture all the students are men – women are cordoned off in an upper part to the right.

73. *Destruction by fire of the Park Theatre*, in Parkway. From the *Penny Illustrated Paper* 17 September 1881. The Mother Red Cap is to the far right.

Music Halls and Melodrama

THE PARK THEATRE

Three theatres have been built in Camden Town. The first, known originally as the Alexandra, was short-lived. It was built on the site of today's Parkway Cinema Centre in 1873. The thespian fare was very much of the period – quite short dramatic or operatic pieces of, probably, no dramatic or literary merit. It became the Royal Park Theatre and when it was burnt down in 1881 the Royal Park Hall was built in its stead, a place which staged plays, provided a home for public meetings and so on. After the 1st World War it appears to have been empty and in the 1930s a Gaumont Cinema was built on its site, later becoming the Odeon and lately the Parkway Centre.

74. Theatre programme for Park Theatre for 1879.

ROYAL
PARK THEATRE,
PARK STREET, CAMDEN TOWN.
Lessees & Managers   Messrs. JOHN and RICHARD DOUGLASS, Park.

MISS LYDIA THOMPSON

MR. LIONEL BROUGH,

AND

Full Company from the Folly Theatre,

FOR SIX NIGHTS ONLY

Commencing MONDAY, March 17th.

The performance will commence each evening at 7.15 o'clock, with the Favourite Patter Farce,

Cryptoconchoidsyphonostomata.

In which Mr CHARLES COLLETTE and Miss BLANCHE WILTON will sustain their Original Characters.

THE GREAT SOUTHERN SABLE MINSTRELS IN CONJUNCTION WITH **SYLVESTER PANTO,** From New York, the most extraordinary Dancer in the World. WILL GIVE TWO GRAND **CONCERTS** AT THE **Camden Literary and Scientific Institution, KING STREET, CAMDEN TOWN,** On Tuesday & Wednesday Evenings. April 7th and 8th, 1857.

During the Entertainments they will sing Selections from their celebrated Programme, including many Original Songs and Pieces, brought by them from the United States of America; which Songs and Pieces being Copyright, can be sung by no other Artistes

PROGRAMME.
PART FIRST.
GRAND OVERTURE—" Vampo's Medley" - - BAND.
REFRAIN—" Commence ye Niggers all" (Original.)
BALLAD—" Emma Snow" - - (New)
QUICK STEP—" Sturm Maresh Galop"
TRIO—" De Three Gardeners"
SOLO—BONES - " Railroad Imitations" (Original)
Which has caused the greatest sensation throughout the United States of America, and pronounced by the Press a Wonderful Performance. This Solo gives an exact representation of preparing the engine before attaching to the train; the starting of the train; its peculiar sound going underneath the tunnels; also crossing the bridges; and its gradual decrease of speed before stopping at the stations.
DUETTO—" I do lub my Dinah"   (New)
AN INTERVAL OF FIVE MINUTES.

PART SECOND.
GRAND DUET—" Instrumental"
SOLO—Banjo—" Virginnia Bells"
Duet—"Double Extraordinary Violin Extravaganza"

75. Not all entertainment was in the theatres and pubs. The Camden Literary and Scientific Institution in Plender Street was also used, this time for a Black and White Minstrel show in 1857.

THE BEDFORD THEATRE

At the turn of this century two theatres were built in Camden Town. The entertainment they provided sends many people nowadays into bouts of nostalgia for an art form which they probably wouldn't have gone to see at the time and would not bother with now if it were available in plenty. However, old wood-type playbills do tend to soften the critical assessment.

In the 1820s the Bedford Tavern and its tea gardens provided entertainment. Fields surrounded it, and a day in the country and a diversion at the Bedford must have been a pleasant way of spending some time. There was a bowling green, there were concerts, and there were arbours.

The Bedford Music Hall arrived in 1861, unnoticed, incidentally, by the standard history of the area published thirteen years later. One of its problems was that it had a very limited frontage on to the High Street – its official address was actually Arlington Road behind, and it was approached from the High Street down a narrow alley parallel to Mary's Terrace. A magazine called *The Era* described

the Bedford then as a 'small and inconvenient building, entered only from a court that ran between the High-street, Camden-town, and the Arlington-road'.

This drawback was overcome on rebuilding when nos. 93 and 95 High Street were demolished to make way for a more imposing entrance. The same magazine described its Italian marble steps in a spacious entrance hall, gilded ceiling and walls, and a floor of marble mosaic. The auditorium met with special approval. It had no columns to interrupt the view, and had handsome private boxes approached by little marble staircases from the stalls. Lighting was by electricity with gas and oil-lamps as standby.

The new theatre opened on 6 February 1899. Its basic fare was light, mainly variety and music hall, in which great names such as Marie Lloyd and George Robey performed. Marie Lloyd played there on her fiftieth birthday and the stage was 'a garden of flowers'.

In January 1907 was heard the last performance of a minor artiste called Belle Elmore, better known as Mrs Crippen. That evening she sang a song called 'Down Lovers' Walk' and what was known as a

76. *Programme for the Bedford Theatre of Varieties.*

tually that the Bedford, for whatever reasons, had had its day as a theatre.

The last performance in the theatre was in 1951; demolition began in 1968, but the final vestiges remained until 1982, when the present Abbey National building was erected. Oddly, for a theatre which had such a lacklustre history, its interior is recorded quite well, first in many of Sickert's drawings, secondly in photographs of the derelict interior before demolition, and third in the film *Trottie True*, starring Jean Kent, some of which was filmed in the Bedford.

77. Belle Elmore.

'coon' song. In costume she sang a song called 'The Major' and also appeared in a musical duologue. That week there was a strike by music hall artists in aid of higher wages and improved conditions. Belle Elmore crossed the picket line, even past Marie Lloyd who remarked that it was best to let her through as she (Belle) would soon empty the house.

After the 1st World War music hall declined and in 1933 the building was leased to Associated British Cinemas for the rest of the thirties.

The Bedford, like other theatres, had to pick itself up in the dreadful recession and depression after the 2nd World War, although it is not clear why cinema, which enjoyed great popularity then, was not using the building. Repertory was tried in 1947, variety was embraced in 1948 and then, quite surprisingly, Donald Wolfit took it over for a season of Shakespeare. Financially, this was not a success.

The next lessee was Pat Nye. Her first production was *Lady Audley's Secret*, starring Anne Crawford. At the gala opening George Robey arrived by stage coach, and in the audience were Laurence Olivier, Jean Simmons, Glynis Johns and Bransby Williams. But despite the occasional appearance of a big name, such as Dirk Bogarde, and the direction of a new play by the young Ken Tynan, the new management, hard though it tried, had to concede even-

78. Bedford Theatre programme, March 1931.

79. *The Bedford Theatre* derelict and awaiting demolition.

80. *Lady Audley's Secret* at the Bedford Theatre in 1949.

81. *Camden Theatre c*1905.

82. *The Camden Theatre* and the junction with Crowndale Road, 1910. Oil painting, artist unknown. The corner shop is Moore's, a baker's; a few doors down is Leverton's the funeral directors. The site was eventually taken by the Post Office for a sorting office and is now mainly used by the Crowndale Centre.

THE CAMDEN THEATRE

The Camden Theatre was opened in December 1900 by Ellen Terry who, as a girl, had lived just down the road in Stanhope Street: *Cinderella* was the first production and Miss Terry's appearance at the opening is still marked by a plaque in the foyer. The architect was William Sprague, designer of so many London theatres. The Camden was considered the finest theatre in the suburbs; certainly it was one of the largest, because it held at least 3,000 people.'The new theatre at once strikes the visitor as a lofty and commanding edifice,' wrote one journalist and, fortunately, it still does in its new role as the Camden Palace nightclub. A marble staircase led to a crush room furnished with deep red upholstery and decorated by Waring & Gillow in the then popular style of Louis XIV.

The *St Pancras Gazette* was fulsome in its praise of the musical *The Geisha* in 1901: 'On Monday the ever-popular *Geisha* commenced on a too-brief run of six nights at the Camden Theatre, and has had a week of most gratifying success. It is a matter for special gratification that the opera was presented at our beautiful local theatre on a scale of magnificence and completeness which would do credit to a West End theatre, but this is nothing new at the Camden Theatre, being rather a continuation of the policy with which the proprietors started their enterprise, viz. to offer nothing to their patrons but standard work, which has received the unmistakeable approval of critics and public.' No fringe theatre there.

By 1924 the Camden was in use as a cinema and it probably survives today only because the BBC took it over from 1945 until 1972, the very period in which similar buildings were demolished without much opposition.

83. *Camden Theatre programme*, June 1903.

THE SILVER SCREEN

As will be seen above both the major theatres, the Bedford and the Camden, succumbed to cinema conversion between the wars. There were, however, some purpose-built cinemas.

By 1911 The Electric Cinema, sometimes called The Britannia, was functioning on the site of the Camden Plaza. After the 1st World War the Electric Palladium traded briefly at 143–145 Camden High Street before the site was taken by Marks & Spencer, who had outgrown their premises to the south. In the 1930s the Gaumont replaced some shops in Parkway and, as we have seen, was coincidentally on the site of the old Park Theatre of Victorian times; this cinema became the Odeon and is presently the Parkway Cinema Centre.

The bingo hall in Delancey Street has seen some of the public's fancies in its day. It was once a cinema called the Fan and then the Dara, and before that it was a billiard rooms.

Artists in their Quarters

THE CAMDEN TOWN GROUP

The Camden Town Group of painters, an association formed in 1911, and its predecessor, the Fitzroy Street Group, have been both influential and enduringly popular. Walter Richard Sickert was prominent in both.

Sickert returned to England in 1905 and rented lodgings at 6 Mornington Crescent, by then an unfashionable address, with trains at the bottom of his garden. He was returning to an old stamping ground, for during the 1890s he had produced numerous sketches and paintings which depicted events at the Bedford Music Hall. He was also re-turning to another reminder – the Cobden statue outside Mornington Crescent station was of his former father-in-law. Sickert seems to have liked railways outside his back garden, for he later had a studio, as we have seen, at the old Wellington House Academy at 247 Hampstead Road, and he also ran a studio and school at Highbury Fields, Islington, which backed on to the North London Line. Certainly, as William Rothenstein was to comment, he had a penchant for seediness.

In 1904 Sickert was introduced to Spencer Gore and thereby into a circle which included Wyndham Lewis, Harold Gilman and Augustus John. By 1907 six painters – Sickert, Gore, Rothenstein and his brother Albert, Walter Russell and Gilman, were renting a first floor at 19 Fitzroy Street. The Fitzroy Street Group was in business. It was not just an informal friendship of artists: it had an organisation and a number of co-operative purposes.

These were startling times in the art world. Not only was the ruling London art world suddenly

84. *Mornington Crescent* by Spencer Gore, *c*1911. In fact not much of the Crescent is visible, but in the distance is the Camden Theatre and Mornington Crescent station. The tower of St Matthew's, Oakley Square, now demolished, is over the rooftops.

85. *Walter Richard Sickert* in 1940. Photograph by Cecil Beaton.

embarrassed to find that it had a good many innovative artists on its hand, but it was scandalised at the introduction by Roger Fry of Post-Impressionists such as Gaugin, Van Gogh and Cézanne. In 1911 remnants of the Fitzroy Street Group decided to form a new society (Walter Bayes is said to have chosen the name) called the Camden Town Group. It was resolved that it should number no more than sixteen and to contain no women. Most of the painters, such as Gore, Sickert, Bevan and Ginner dealt with urban life; but new members such as Epstein broadened its spectrum.

In 1913 the Camden and Fitzroy groups merged, to form the London Group, but it was immediately beset by personal differences and in 1914 both Sickert and Pissarro resigned. Like all good artistic movements, the Camden Town Group did not last long and just withered away when its original leaders left.

CAMDEN TOWN STUDIOS

Three sets of studios have existed in Camden Town. The oldest, and the least known, was in Camden Road on the site of the present Sainsbury building. There were six studios and they were occupied from at least 1876 by artists now unfamiliar to us. The studios were still there in 1904 and were probably demolished to make way for the ABC building.

The better-known Camden Town Studios were in Camden Street, but again they housed no artist of note today. There were nine studios usually occupied by artists until the Borough Council redevelopment of the area in the 1960s. New studios were built by the Council to replace them, together with an exhibition hall whose largest door was too small to get large paintings through. But as so happens when something is planned, the mix of local authority and artists did not work. Once the best-known artist there, Peter Peri, had died, hardly any cachet remained.

In Cliff Road, in the extreme east of Camden Town, some studios were built after the last war. They still survive and are generally used by artists. Naum Gabo, the Russian constructivist, had the studio at present used by the sculptor Ghisha Koenig.

PRIMROSE HILL STUDIOS

Concealed behind Fitzroy Road in Chalk Farm is a group of twelve studios which were begun in 1877. They were built and designed by Alfred Healey, a local builder and property owner with offices in Princess Road, whose father had speculated on the development of the Crown Estate off Regent's Park.

An unusual feature was that the studios were provided with a lodge whose keeper and wife supervised the cleaning and even provided main meals. This arrangement continued until the 1940s and was described in Joseph Hutton's *By Order of the Czar* as similar to that of an old-fashioned College or Inn.

The best-known occupants of the studios have been Arthur Rackham, the illustrator, and Henry Wood, the conductor. The studios are still rented out to artists and, according to the Property Trust which owns them, there is a waiting list.

86. *The toll gate at Mornington Crescent c*1860. Many toll gates, including this one, were abolished in 1864. Part of its site was taken for the Cobden Statue.

The Cobden Statue

One of the least convincing statues in London is that of Richard Cobden, outside Mornington Crescent station. It was, unfortunately, done on the cheap, and shows it.

Cobden was an oddity in English politics. Though one of the most successful politicians of his period, he neither obtained nor sought high office. In those days of loose political coalitions he could be admired and befriended by all parties, and indeed he was. In particular he was popular with the general public. His campaign to abolish the Corn Laws which artificially held up the price of corn in a country where the poor were sometimes on the verge of starvation, was a model of its kind. He used new methods of rousing public opinion, spectacular fund-raising events, using even the new penny post to canvass every voter. Devoted to the principal of free trade among nations he travelled extensively and became friendly with many rulers, Napoleon III among them.

Why Camden Town was chosen for his principal statue is unclear. A group of local admirers seem to have had the idea, and the site was available when the old toll gate was removed. From these men developed a memorial committee which obtained the Vestry's permission to raise the statue. The *Building News* of the time commented: 'To the parish of St Pancras will belong the credit and the honour of raising the first public memorial to the memory of the late Richard Cobden, MP, in the metropolis.'

The statue was commissioned from W & T Wills of Euston Road, and it was decided that Cobden's stance should be that of speaking in Parliament. This was in 1865, but there were numerous delays and there was a shortage of money – nothing disappears so quickly as gratitude to a politician. Not until 1868 was the inauguration possible, and this was performed not by someone of the ilk of Gladstone, but by the two local Members of Parliament.

Cobden's widow, Catherine, and her daughters,

87. *The unveiling of the Cobden Statue* on 27 June 1868. To the right is the North London Collegiate School for Boys – a number of pupils may be seen leaning out of the windows.

came up for the day to see the ceremony and she was hosted by a surgeon who lived in a house on the site of Mornington Crescent underground station. One journal was very sniffy about the ceremony, saying that the crowd attending was rather scruffy, but the early photograph shown here does not reinforce that opinion. Most interestingly, this picture by Henry Dixon of Albany Street shows the east side of the High Street where the buildings stretching up from today's Camden Palace are still premises with gardens in front. Boys can be seen looking out of the window of the North London Collegiate School for Boys on the right.

The Famous Residents

WRITERS

We have already mentioned the Charles DICKENS local connections – see p67. H.G. WELLS (1866–1946) had several Camden Town and Chalk Farm addresses. He did, of course, have the invaders in *The War of the Worlds* land, and eventually expire, on Primrose Hill, a place he was familiar with, because in 1889–91 he boarded with his aunt at no. 46 Fitzroy Road, while he was assistant master at Henley House School, Kilburn. But he also lived at 7 Mornington Place (a terrace in Hampstead Road) in 1894 and then moved to no. 12 Mornington Terrace for four years; here he lived with his mistress, Catherine Robbins, and wrote *The Time Machine* and *The Island of Dr Moreau*. William Butler YEATS (1865–

1939), Irish poet and dramatist, was at no. 23 Fitzroy Road when he was a small boy, before his return to Ireland. More recently Sylvia PLATH (1932–63), the American poet, was at the same address; it was here that she committed suicide in 1963. Previously she and her husband, poet Ted HUGHES (*b*1930), lived around the corner at no. 7 Chalcot Square. Another poet in Chalcot Square was Isaac ROSENBERG (1890–1918), at no. 1.

Alfred Lord TENNYSON (1809–92), lodged in 1850 at no. 25 Mornington Place, a house whose site is now covered by the block of flats called Silverdale. When he moved out of the house he accidentally left behind the manuscript of his famous poem *In Memoriam* which, fortunately, Coventry Patmore was able to retrieve before it was lost. Opposite, in the now truncated Harrington Square, the writer, E.V. LUCAS (1868–1938), lived in 1892.

Off the High Street at 54 Delancey Street lived Dylan THOMAS (1914–53), the poet, in 1951–52; he had access to a caravan in the back garden here. He didn't much care for the situation. He wrote 'Our

88. *Dylan Thomas*, his landlady and caravan, in the garden at 54 Delancey Street, *c*1952.

89. *William Butler Yeats* (1861–1939). Charcoal drawing by J.S. Sargent.

90. *Spencer Gore* (1878–1914), self-portrait, 1914.

new London house of horror on bus and night lorry route and opposite railway bridge and shunting station'. He did use the library in Camden Street and was owing three books to the council when he died. Charlotte MEW (1869–1928), poet, was at what was no. 86 Delancey Street in 1922–26. Her life was one of much frustration, both sexual and artistic, and much of it was spent nursing her mother and then her sister, Anne. Only one volume of her poems – Thomas Hardy thought very highly of her – was published during her lifetime. Charlotte Mew left the house in Delancey Street in 1926 to nurse her sister, who soon died of cancer. This unhinged Charlotte who, in a nursing home in 1928, committed suicide by drinking disinfectant. In Regent's Park Road the novelist, Nigel BALCHIN (1908–70), lived at no. 48 from 1960 until his death in 1970.

ARTISTS

Patrick CAULFIELD was in Primrose Hill Studios by 1981 and Paul HOGARTH lived in both Princess Road and Manley Street.

Spencer GORE (1878–1914), a member of the Camden Town Group, was at Granby Terrace in 1907, at 31 Mornington Crescent in 1909, and across the road after his marriage in 1912 at 2 Houghton Place: Sickert, his friend, is mentioned on p82. William Powell FRITH (1819–1909), a favourite large-canvas painter of the Victorians was at no. 13 Park Village East. Numerous engravers have worked in Camden Town, the most notable being Francis HOLL (1815–84), who was born in Bayham Street in 1815, and is noted in Gloucester Avenue in 1879. The DALZIEL family, famous for their innovations in reproduction techniques, were at several addresses in the area. George CRUIKSHANK (1792–1878), the illustrator, lived at what was then 48 Mornington Place and is now no. 263 Hampstead Road, from 1850. The gifted ceramicist, William de MORGAN (1839–1917), was at no. 15 Camden Street in 1844–55 and Lawrence ALMA-TADEMA (1836–1912) lived at 4 Camden Square in 1871.

Until recently Henry SELOUS (1801–90), artist, was commemorated by a Camden Town street name. He was exhibited at the Royal Academy while at addresses in Bayham Street, Camden Street and Gloucester Avenue and also at what is now Keats House in Hampstead. Unfortunately for his topographical posterity, his brother, Frederick Courtney Selous, a modest man by all accounts, was, however, largely responsible for the indiscriminate and quite often barbaric colonialisation and parcelling up of southern Africa; when the Anti-Apartheid Movement took premises in Selous Street it was felt appropriate to change the street name to Mandela Street. It is an odd coincidence that the farm just down the road from Selous Street, just behind the site of Mornington Crescent station, was tenanted by Thomas Rhodes, who was related to Cecil Rhodes the African explorer with whom Frederick Selous achieved notoriety. The artistic work of the now dispossessed Henry Selous is little known today, but a large picture by him of Queen Victoria may be seen at the V & A Museum, in the Victorian furniture gallery.

POLITICIANS

Friedrich ENGELS (1820–95), political writer and close friend of Karl Marx, lived at no. 122 Regent's Park Road, where there is now a blue plaque. Engels lived successively here with two Irish sisters, both of whom became his common law wives; however, he married the second sister by special licence just before her death here. Marx was not far away, across the road from Chalk Farm in the Queen's Crescent area, and would certainly have faced financial ruin had it not been for the support of his friend. Engels died soon after moving to no. 41 in the same road.

Two famous 'patriots' have lived in the area. Louis KOSSUTH (1802–94), of Hungary, was at 12 Regent's Park Terrace in 1861, and José RIZAL (1861–96), of the Phillipines, was at no. 37 Chalcot Crescent in 1888–89. Both were prominent in independence struggles in their own countries. Rizal had come to England in 1888, when he was 27, to research in the archives of the British Museum the lost history of the Filipinos, so as to justify their independence. His research and ideas led to the Phillipine Revolution in 1896. Equally instrumental, but in another country, was the Indian, Krishna MENON (1896–1974), who was a member of the St Pancras Council from 1934 until 1948, and a difficult associate of Nehru and Gandhi in the fight for Indian independence. Menon lived in penurious circumstances at 57 Camden Square from 1924 until 1947. Not so well known was his collaboration with Allen Lane in beginning Penguin Books. Menon was made a Freeman of the borough in 1955.

91. *Krishna Menon* at the ceremony in 1955 in which he received the Freedom of St Pancras Borough.

PANORAMIC PICTURE OF THE FUNERAL OF TOM SAYERS.

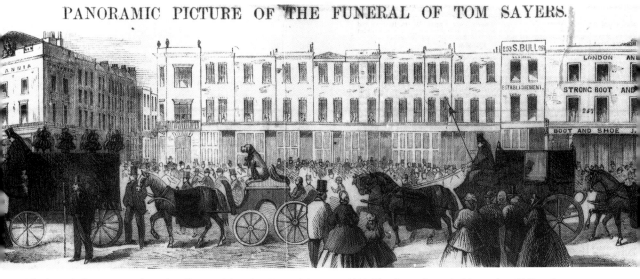

92. *The funeral of Tom Sayers* from the *Illustrated Sporting News* 13 January 1866. The funeral was in November 1865 and streets were cleared to make way for the enormous procession from Camden Street up to Highgate Cemetery. His famous dog (captured in stone on the Sayers grave at Highgate) is the second main attraction of the event. The artist's topography is rather inaccurate. The Britannia pub at the south corner of Parkway and the High Street is visible to the left, and the shops to the right can only be those leading up to Inverness Street. However, the numbering is all wrong, since no. 253, for example, is to the north of Inverness Street, which does not appear in the illustration. Even more to the point, the procession is going the wrong way for Highgate Cemetery.

SCIENTISTS

Sir William CROOKES (1832–1919), scientist, lived at no. 20 Mornington Terrace until he moved to Kensington in 1880. Sir Oliver LODGE (1851–1940), physicist, was in rooms at no. 62 Delancey Street from 1874–77 while he was studying at University College. He lived in Harrington Square after his marriage. Oliver HEAVISIDE (1850–1925), another physicist, was born at what was then no. 55 Plender Street, the son of a wood engraver and watercolour artist. He later lived at no. 117 Camden Road and 3 St Augustine's Road.

DEATH OF A PUGILIST

Few pugilists have managed to get into the *Dictionary of National Biography*. Tom SAYERS (1826–65) lived and fought hard, died young, and achieved sufficient notoriety to join the famous. Though quite small – less than 5′ 9′ – he had great power in his fists and neck muscles. His only defeat was in a fight which lasted for sixty-one rounds and went on for just over two hours. But his most famous contest, and the one which endeared him to the sports followers of the day, was against the American champion, Jim Heenan, in 1860, which lasted for over two hours six minutes and led to an inconclusive result, since the contest was declared a draw. Sayers died in 1865 and was buried in Highgate Cemetery after a vast procession had walked from Camden Town to Highgate. At the time of his death he was living at no. 51 Camden Street.

93. *The Mother Red Cap*. A naive representation of the road junction. Brown's Dairy is to the left and the Halfway House pub is in the centre.

Old Drinking Places

RED CAP AND BLACK CAP

The age of the name 'Mother Red Cap', its origin, and the reason why it was applied to the predecessors of the large pub in Camden Town now called the World's End, are not known. Equally puzzling is the name 'Mother Black Cap', which still survives.

The first reference to an alehouse or tavern in the area occurs in the parish registers for 5 Sep 1690. Walter Langley is recorded as being buried 'from the Halfway House', a name which was used for a dwelling by the Camden Town fork to Hampstead and Kentish Town for many years. In October 1703 a highwayman was 'shott to death' near the Halfway House and was buried without the service of the Church. The same year Richard George, cowkeeper and victualler at the Halfway House in the Hampstead Road, was buried. But also the same

year we have a man called John Meaking, a chocolate maker of London, dying at 'Mother Damnable's' in Kentish Town. This name appears to have been later occasionally used instead of Mother Red Cap; the following year, 1704, the registers record the death of Margaret Bartholomew, a widow, who kept an alehouse at Mother Damnable's.

It is unclear from these entries if the Halfway House and Mother Damnable's are one and the same thing, or separate buildings, or if either one of them went on for certain to become Mother Red Cap.

The licensing records are even less helpful. From 1723–35 there is a Halfway House listed, then there is a break until 1751 when appears both a Mother Red Cap and a Mother Black Cap. Rocque's map of 1746, a few years earlier, has the words 'Old Mother Red Caps' (note the plural) spread out over the junction of roads, but it is not clear at which building he is pointing. It should be said, just to confuse matters even further, that another Mother Red Cap existed in the Holloway Road – this is mentioned in a mid–17th century book and is also known to have issued a trade token during the Restoration period when coinage was short. This establishment, too,

94. *The College Arms* at the junction of Royal College Street and Crowndale Road, *c*1905. This has now been replaced by a modern building.

was called Halfway House. It was situated, as it still is, at the northern end of Holloway Road but it is not known what it was halfway between.

We are on firmer ground, however, in Camden Town from 1751. The Mother Black Cap was then on the site of the present underground station, because we know it was bought in 1778 by the Vestry for use as a workhouse. There is then a break of three years until the Black Cap appears again, this time on its present site in the High Street. A continuous record of both public houses is available from this period.

But who was Mother Damnable or Red Cap? The most popular legend is that the name derives from a woman called Jinney, daughter of a Kentish Town brickmaker, who had several husbands that died in mysterious circumstances. There is, though, no evidence for the legend.

The oldest *named* pub in Camden Town was at the bottom of Royal College Street. It appears in the court rolls for 1705 when Henry George was admitted to his late brother's property the George and Falcon 'at the end of Figg Lane [Crowndale Road] by St Pancras Church'. Quite possibly the 'George' part of the name derived from its owner. This inn later became the Elephant and Castle and was demolished to make way for Goldington Court.

95. *Chalk Farm Tavern* in the 1820s, probably by T.H. Shepherd.

96. *Chalk Farm Tavern* in the 1840s.

THE CHALK FARM TAVERN

The Chalk Farm Tavern appears for certain in the 1732 licensing records as Chalk House Farm. It has been suggested (see p17) that it was the White House to which the body of Sir Edmund Godfrey was carried after its discovery on Primrose Hill. If so, it was no more than an alehouse, with 'no accommodation, nor hangings, nor scarce a window.' From 1760 the place was called the Stag and Hounds: an advertisement of 1785 describes it as having 80 acres of farmland tenanted by Thomas Rhodes, with three large barns.

From 1790, under the management of Thomas Rutherford, the place became known to a wider public. At the Chalk Farm Tavern and Tea Gardens 'T. Rutherford solicits the patronage of the Public in general – his wines being real and his other liquors of a superior kind. Tea and hot rolls as usual. An ordinary [a set meal] on Sundays at Two o'clock.' It should be noted that the word 'tavern' had a precise meaning at that time. Beer *and* wine could be sold, but there was no accommodation.

At that time Primrose Hill Road did not exist and the gardens of the tavern were contiguous with Primrose Hill; they also stretched across Regent's Park Road and were contained in the half circle encompassed today by Sharpleshall Street and Berkley Road. The views illustrated here of the 1830s and 1840s show that the modest tavern had grown into a substantial enterprise. The building was demolished in 1853 and rebuilt the following year as that which survives in Regent's Park Road today. It boasted a 'Chinese Orchestra' which was a bandstand, and a dance floor able to take a thousand people. The pub was owned by brewers called Calvert, who are remembered in a local street name, and who also opened a new pub in the area called The Engineer.

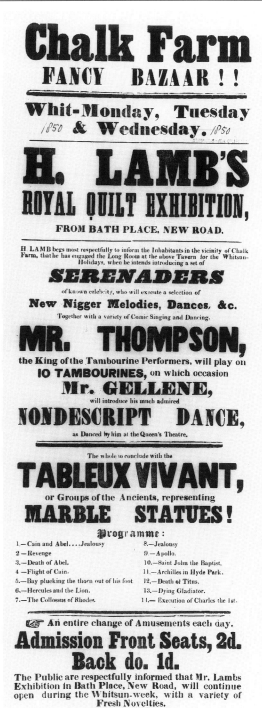

97. Advertisement for a bazaar held at the Chalk Farm Tavern in 1850.

98. Advertisement for the Edinburgh Castle Free Museum.

THE EDINBURGH CASTLE

One local pub which attained some degree of fame was the Edinburgh Castle in Mornington Terrace. In the late 19th century the proprietor, Thomas Middlebrook, established here a museum of curiosities of the sort beloved of Victorians. The exhibits included relics of Lord Nelson, the egg of a Great Auk bird (which cost 180 guineas), a gold medal given by the British government to the Rajah of Mysore, a 4,000-year-old Babylonian brick and a 14th-century mother-of-pearl picture. When the contents were sold in 1908 the catalogue claimed a bugle which (allegedly) sounded the charge at the Battle of Balaklava, and a collection of 80,000 butterflies.

FISTICUFFS AND OTHER SPORTS

Pub sports are quieter affairs nowadays. In the 18th century remote taverns were the venues for duels and other kinds of needle matches. In 1786 'a very desperate boxing match was fought between two noted London bruisers in a field near the Mother Red Cap'. The contest lasted upwards of fifty minutes when the person supposed to be victor received a blow from his antagonist in the stomach 'which laid him for dead.'

The upper class sport of duelling was familiar at Chalk Farm. Contests in 1803 and 1818 were between army personnel and one, in 1821, was a civil

99. *Lt. Munro*, eventually brought to trial

100. *The Brecknock Arms*, Camden Road in 1856.

101. *Duelling at Chalk Farm.*

quarrel. In each of them one of the participants died. It is claimed that the last old-fashioned duel in this country, (though it would be difficult to decide what was a formal duel and what a straightforward fight) was fought at the Brecknock Arms in Camden Road in 1843. A Lt Munro challenged Colonel Fawcett, his brother-in-law, and it was the latter who received a gunshot wound.

Unusually, for such a rural area, a police constable was nearby and soon on the scene. He found three men, one bleeding from a wound in the chest. On the constable asking what had happened, the injured man said "What is it to you? It was an accident." Unfortunately the landlord of the Brecknock was away, his wife was in bed, and the waiter flatly refused to take in the wounded man, and so he was carried down to the Camden Arms in Randolph Street, where he died two days later. At the inquest the jury was made up of fourteen residents of Cam-

den Town, and the coroner was Thomas Wakley, the founder of the magazine *The Lancet*. It was not until 1847 that Munro was brought to trial and by then public indignation had subsided; he received a year's imprisonment.

The Brecknock Arms was the centre of a less hazardous contest in 1840. A Notice proclaimed: 'A Grand Pedestrian Match for £500 at the Brecknock Arms. Harris the celebrated and unrivalled pedestrian, has been backed by Messrs Clark, Parr, Jenkins and Pernell, to perform the Herculean task of walking 1750 miles in 1000 hours, being 1¾ miles every successive hour, in a measured circle in the Bowling Green and Tea Gardens of the above Tavern. The Pedestrian will commence walking on Monday, Sep 21st at 8 o'clock in the morning and will continue walking every hour throughout the Day and Night without variation or intermission.'

102. *The Railway Tavern*, Chalk Farm Road, 1905. Champagne is advertised at 6d a glass.

CAMDEN ESTATE
CAMDEN TOWN.

Particulars, Plans and Conditions of Sale of

THE FREEHOLD INTEREST

IN SEVERAL

LARGE BLOCKS OF PROPERTY

FORMING

VALUABLE BUILDING SITES

Of 1¼ Acres   1 Acre and ¾ Acre

IN KING'S ROAD.

SEVERAL OTHERS OF LESSER AREA

IN GREAT COLLEGE STREET   CAMDEN ROAD
CAMDEN STREET   KENTISH TOWN ROAD

FOUR FULLY-LICENSED PUBLIC HOUSES

"THE FALCON"   "THE OLD EAGLE"
"THE EAGLE" and   "THE PRINCE ALBERT"

TOGETHER WITH

WHARVES ON THE REGENT'S CANAL, NUMEROUS SHOPS, FACTORY PREMISES, HOUSES AND OTHER PROPERTIES

in the immediate neighbourhood of **CAMDEN TOWN STATION.**

TOTAL GROSS ASSESSMENT about

£23,000 per annum.

With POSSESSION at MICHAELMAS, 1919, and at later dates.

103. In 1919 The Camden Estate sold out its freehold interest in properties between Royal College Street and Camden Street. These included the Lawford wharf and four pubs. The Prince Albert, the pub in Royal College Street with the attractive green fascia tiles, went for £440 at the auction. This price was marked on the sale catalogue belonging to the proprietor of Lawford's, who declined to buy the wharf his company occupied that day, at what was retrospectively seen as a bargain price.

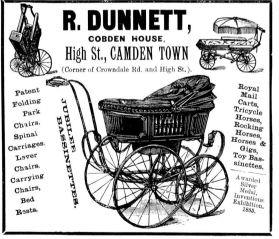

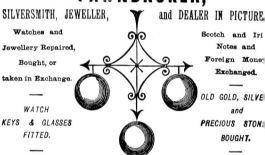
104. A selection of small advertisements of Camden Town traders.

The Traders

BEFORE THE CHAIN STORES

Camden High Street has always been a shopping street for essentials, usually sold in the 'pile 'em high and sell 'em cheap' fashion. If modern gentrification has changed the nearby housing stock it has not had the same effect on the main shopping street, which remains much as it was. In essence the atmosphere of the street is of a market, with wares outside. A street market did in fact exist in the High Street on certain days between the wars – Plender Street is probably the rump of that, and Inverness Market appears to have been going before the 1st World War.

The most sought-after plots in the High Street were and still are those just south and just north of Parkway. Unusually, the side of the road which gets the most sun has been the least popular.

The day of the small business was at its height in Camden Town towards the end of the nineteenth century. Only one chain store was in the area, the Home & Colonial, a grocery business whose dignified gilt letters were once familiar in every high street. The company is now part of Lipton's, itself one of the earliest multiples in Camden High Street. Up and down the road little businesses, from coal-merchants to wardrobe dealers, were to be seen, many of them frozen for posterity by the fact that when the underground railway was built in the first few years of the next century it was thought that a comprehensive photographic survey should be made so as to avoid spurious claims for damage and subsidence. That range of photographs, of such brilliant clarity that the prices of goods in the windows may be easily read, are in the Local Studies Library, and are the most evocative way of examining retail trade at that time.

On the site of the underground station itself stood Brown's Dairy. The proprietor claimed that the business was founded in about 1790, but we know not where; it was here on this corner by 1822 but the name does not occur in local records before that. The premises it occupied, known as the 'Cows'

105. *Brown's Dairy* Camden Town. The 'Cows' Cathedral', as it was called, stood on the site of the Underground station.

106. The shop of J.A. Lake at 33 Camden High Street, 1877. The public are looking at a wall poster printed by the *British Workman*, entitled 'Judge Payne's Short Sermon'. A jewellers still exists at this address and the present proprietor is hoping to restore the shop front to nearer its original form.

Cathedral', were remarkable and are shown on p99. When the underground railway was built Brown's moved in 1903 to what is now the derelict no. 6 Parkway, taking over the original ABC bakery. In the High Street, opposite the site of the underground station, were two large drapery businesses, of the kind that in many towns and, indeed, in Oxford Street, developed into department stores. At 197–203 were Nicholson and Wordley, and at 205–209 was Broadhead's, both of them linen drapers. Much of the site and eventually all of it was taken by Marshall Roberts, drapers and general store, by 1907, and later on by the Co-op. South of these on the later Woolworth site was Pugh's, another large drapers.

The most important store in Camden Town was undoubtedly that of Bowman Brothers. Not only was it the largest, drawing in custom from miles around because of its wide selection of furniture, but it also had the effect, seen in retrospect, of blighting the east side of the road. Towards the end of the century when shopping patterns were beginning to change and multiples were appearing with a more professional retailing approach, the prime sites on the east side of the road were already taken by Bowman. So it was that the west side eventually got the multiples.

Thomas and Robert Bowman, sons of a Lakeland

Highest Award,
Laundry Exhibition,
1895.

Telephone No.
1633 North.

ST. JAMES'S LAUNDRY.

"Right in the Front."

St. James's Laundry,
67, CAMDEN ROAD, N.W.,
—— Near North London Railway.

For Private Families.
Dyeing and Cleaning in all its branches.
Feathers cleaned, dyed and curled.

108. Advertisement for St James's Laundry in Camden Road, from a 1907 Directory.

107. Bowman Brothers store c1905.

farming family, established an upholstery business at no. 108 High Street in 1864. Four years later Robert resigned the partnership leaving Thomas to develop it. Thomas was astute enough to trade in furniture at a time when mass-produced items could be produced cheaply for a burgeoning middle-class. Mahogany was king just as pine is now; brass bedsteads were usual, bathrooms though not usual were mostly boxed in mahogany and marbled; there were plenty of items for reclining in – divans, ottomans, chesterfields and sofas.

In typical Victorian fashion Bowman extended his business in a hotchpotch of adjacent shops, a situation resolved in 1893 when some caught fire; they were rebuilt as the gabled building familiar to modern eyes. Trade declined in the 1970s and '80s and the old business has now gone.

Another firm of furnishers, Oetzmann's, whose main shop was in the lower part of Hampstead Road, had a cabinet factory in Camden High Street, on the site of the public library, in a building which had once been the North London Collegiate School

109. *The Oetzmann Cabinet Factory* in Camden High Street in 1904. It is the same building as previously used by the North London Collegiate School for Boys (see illustration 87). The Camden Town Library is now on part of the site.

110. *The St Pancras Gazette* premises at 80 Camden High Street in 1904.

for Boys. The firm of Pegram's in Royal College Street, who specialise now in custom-made furniture and shop and office fitting, claim descent from Alfred Pegram who, it is said, began as a cabinet maker in Camden Town in 1860; unfortunately no record of the Pegram business appears in the directories until about 1910.

By 1907 Harold Trill, later to be a St Pancras councillor and mayor (as was his son), had set up his printing and stationery business on the west side of the High Street. This family-run firm lasted until quite recently, but by then was on the east side of the road. Another local printing firm, run by a Mr Widdicombe, also owned the *St Pancras Gazette*, which was printed in the High Street. In 1930 Widdicombe was elected to the St Pancras Council representing the Municipal Reform party, the local name for the Conservative Party. His newspaper had a considerable political bias, carrying news only of Conservative meetings, which makes the assessment of political life at a turbulent period difficult. The *Gazette* later became the *North London Press* whose lineal descendant is the *Camden New Journal*.

Parkway, then known as Park Street, had smaller, more peripheral businesses – sign-writers, booksellers, mantle and costume makers, and Barling's, the tobacco pipe makers. Before the Great War Shand & Co, decorators, were at the Gloucester Gate end; this was a firm later to expand as wallpaper manufacturers in Highgate Road where now carpet factories reign. In the cluster of buildings in the alleyway off the south-west end of Parkway (now splendidly restored) tenants included the celebrated music printers, Lowe & Brydon. On the same side at that time William Heal developed from an ironmonger to a builder, and then when his sons John and Wilfred took over they became J.H. & W. Heal on the other side of the road. This firm, under different ownership today, still survives in Parkway, holding out against the onslaught of boutiques and eating places.

THE LEVERTON BUSINESS

Undoubtedly the oldest ratepayers in Camden are Leverton's, the funeral directors. Their business, which at first included carpentry, has been traced back to 1789, but the Camden Town connection began at the end of 1888 when the firm moved up from the Hampstead Road area to the site of the Crowndale Centre and in 1912 moved down a few doors in Eversholt Street to nos. 210–214. In the early days in Eversholt Street funerals with a single-horse brougham cost 30 shillings (£1.50) plus a 4 shillings (20p) cemetery fee, and those with two

111. *Parkway* (then Park Street) *c*1905. On the left is the stretch of shops running down to Arlington Road.

112. The funeral cortege of Henry Croft, King of the Pearly Kings, in 1930, led by Stanley Leverton. The procession is leaving the southern end of Eversholt Street, turning into Euston Road. It will eventually finish at St Pancras Cemetery in Finchley. The four horses pulling the hearse wear velvets, which will be removed before they begin to trot. Members of the Pearly fraternity walk beside the hearse. To the far left are Pearly Kings and Queens in their own carts.

113. The Annual outing of the employees of J.H. & W. Heal, near their premises in Parkway in c1919. Fred Russell, who contributed this picture, is second from the left on the carriage, with the bowler hat.

horses cost £2.50p. Horses were still being used up to the last war, when some bolted at a funeral during an air raid, and it was thought best to use motors entirely after that. In any case, horses were much slower and by the time they had got to the usual cemetery at Finchley and then come back, most of the day had gone.

The business of undertaking has changed greatly. When Leverton's set up in Camden Town the nature of a funeral was important to all those concerned and the object of curiosity of those who were not. Social status was assessed by the cost of the trappings, so that the poor expended more than they could afford (and still do) on a funeral to persuade others that the family had resources. Most families relied on insurance schemes, taken out by parents when their children were very young – a wise precaution with infant mortality so high. The penny a week insurance was a habit that stuck. Even Stanley Leverton, who was still chairman of the company when he died in 1963, had been persuaded as a younger man by his wife to take out such an insurance even though a free funeral was the most likely perk he would get.

There are other differences now. In the Victorian period the body was usually kept at the house until the funeral; most often now it is kept by the undertaker or is held at a hospital. In the late Victorian period the purchase of the right mourning clothes,

accoutrements and the printing of the appropriate stationery, was catered for by 'mourning warehouses', one of which stood in Camden High Street near to Inverness Street – it was an annexe to the large drapers, Nicholson and Wordley, just south of it. Before the last war one in eleven funerals was a cremation, now four in five are; at the turn of the century neighbours and fellow tradesmen drew curtains on the day of a colleague's funeral, everyone wore black and occasionally undertakers positioned a 'mute' outside the room of the deceased. Nowadays grief is private – only the Cypriot community display it.

Leverton's, incidentally, also had an office next to the Dublin Castle in Parkway where they bought out the premises of Samuel Freshwater and either his wife or daughter, Annie Freshwater, who was a florist. She appears in the story of a Mr Hucks, an aviator, who probably lived at 22 Oval Road, and who was the first man, in 1913, to fly a loop-the-loop. On the day he was to attempt it he called in at her shop and bought a nosegay for luck.

A BUILDERS' MERCHANT IN CAMDEN TOWN

Another Camden Town firm – Lawford's, the builders' merchants, is over a hundred and fifty years old, and is probably the oldest Camden Town

114. The Lawford foreman with horse and cart at the Camden Town wharf in 1923.

115. *Lawford's Wharf from Lyme Terrace*, drawn by G.H. Cook in 1925.

116. A Lawford lorry in 1923.

firm. John Eeles Lawford set up shop in Euston Road in 1840 as a slate merchant and after a few years took up a yard in Royal College Street by the canal. That yard, between Lyme Terrace and Street, is still their's today. It was John Eeles junior who expanded the firm, into Willesden, Edgware, Finchley and Highgate. This John Eeles was also a St Pancras vestryman, elected and re-elected eight times, becoming churchwarden as the culmination of his career in public office. But he must have made some enemies on the way, for when in 1877 the vestry proposed a tribute to him on his death – usually a formality – a vote was demanded and the eulogy was passed 28–2. He was also a developer – Woodsome and Laurier Roads, off Highgate Road, and streets off Kentish Town Road (including Lawford Road) were all developed by him.

The Aerated Bread Company (ABC) began, as we have noted already, at what is now no. 6 Parkway, and then took premises on the present Sainsbury site. The business flourished – not only was it to become one of the largest mass-producing bakeries and part of a conglomerate of similar companies, but it was to launch a chain of tea-shops to compete with the Lyons company. The small bakery in Camden Road was rebuilt as one complex in 1938 by Sir Alexander Gibb, and demolished quite recently to make way for the new Sainsbury store.

A feature of Royal College Street was once the Idris mineral water factory, a firm which had its own artesian well. It was founded by Thomas Howell Idris, who later became prominent on St Pancras Council and the London County Council, and did sufficiently well to finish up with a house in St Alban's Villas at the end of Highgate Road. The Idris firm, which distinguished itself with one of the most banal slogans ever – "I drink Idris when I's dri" – was merged into a soft drinks conglomerate eventually and left Camden Town when that part of Royal College Street was redeveloped.

117. *Nos. 3–5 Camden High Street* in 1904.

118. *Chalk Farm Road c*1905.

119. *Page Bros.* at 229–231 Camden High Street at the beginning of the 20th century.

THE PRESS, at 88, Camden Road. 1862.

Printed by **PREMO PRESS,**
(formerly Warren Hall & Lovitt, Established 1852),
211, GREAT COLLEGE STREET, LONDON, N.W. 1
(Printers to St. Thomas', Agar Town, since 1863).

120. Advertisement for Premo Press in Royal College Street.

121. An unusual advertisement for the North Western Clothing Emporium at 95 Camden High Street.

122. Advertisement for Sydney Jones, pharmacist near Oakley Square. Note the offer of leeches.

123. Parkway in the 1930s. Romano's, a fruiterer, was next door to the Dublin Castle.

Great College Street, Camden Town N. W.

124. The small shopping centre in Royal College Street *c*1905.

125. Trade advertising postcard for A. Mears, jewellers of 73–75 Camden High Street.

**STARTLING
VALUE !**

**Solid Silver
Lever Watch,**

Compensated Balance,
Capped and Jewelled,
and all latest Improve-
ments, Stout, Hall-
marked Silver Cases.

These Splendid
Watches are Extraor-
dinary Value and Per-
fect Reliable Time-
keepers.

A Written Warranty
given for three years.

SPECIAL CASH PRICE

17/6

Post Free to any part
of the World.

A. MEARS & CO.,
73, 75 High Street,
CAMDEN TOWN N.W.
(Estab. Forty Years.)

Series by the Scottish Photographic Touring and Pictorial Post Card Coy., Glasgow.

A NEW SHOPPING ERA

An indication of the new wave of retailing occurs in the Camden Town street directory for 1911. At no. 133 High Street is the London Penny Bazaar Co. This small chain of shops had copied the formula made successful by Michael Marks who had begun, first as a peddler, then as a market-stall holder in Leeds in 1884; he went on to operate 'bazaars' in shops. The retailing features which Marks made popular were firstly, a fixed price on items, so that there was no haggling; secondly, all the merchandise was on display to be looked at and handled – there was no need to ask the shopkeeper to produce something for inspection; thirdly, Marks dealt as far as possible with the manufacturers and cut out middlemen, thereby buying in bulk and selling at the cheapest rates. At the time F.W. Woolworth was doing the same thing in the United States but on a larger scale.

In 1913 Marks & Spencer bought up the London Bazaar Company and took over the Camden Town shop which is henceforth in the directories as 'Marks & Spencer Ltd, bazaar'. To the south of them the site eventually occupied by Woolworth's was still in the hands of small businesses and it was not until the 1930s that the American company appeared.

At the conclusion of the Great War several businesses, still with us today, took root in Camden Town. Montagu Saxby took over a trunk-making business established by Frank Leader at 24 Camden Road. His business there was a familiar sight until recent years when it moved to Kentish Town Road. At the same time Frank Romany, who had had a shop in Soho, opened an ironmongery business on the east side of the High Street. Though the family sold out the firm some five years ago, the shop survives under the same name today and is a familiar haven for those who desperately need a particular kind of bolt or latch on a Saturday afternoon.

A third newcomer in Camden Town at the end of the Great War was George Palmer, who opened up a 'livestock' shop in Parkway, which is still the delight of everyone who passes it. The Regent Pet Shop, opened in 1918, claims to be the oldest pet shop in the world; John Palmer, a descendant of the founder, has only recently retired.

126. Mr and Mrs Frank Romany, who founded and managed the hardware and ironmongery store in Camden High Street

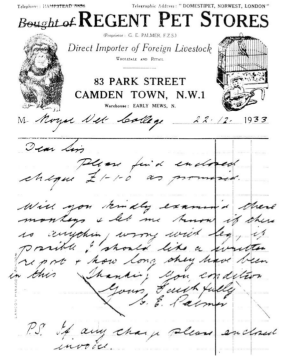

127. (Top) A taxidermist at work in Camden Town. Edward Gerrard and Sons at 61 College Place in the mid-1950s.

128. (Left) A request from the Regent Pet Stores in Parkway to the Royal Veterinary College for help with the treatment of some monkeys.

129. A picture of the King's Road Forge in St Pancras Way shortly before its closure. The picture is interesting for at least two reasons – the original road name and old trade in its title

A New Century

AN UNDERGROUND WORLD

Gillian Tindall in an article in the *Camden History Review* has pointed out that the prosperity of the Victorian years had its darker side in Camden Town. The dirt of industry and railways produced squalor. Poverty brought crime, drunkenness and prostitution as a new, rootless, urban population drifted from one lodging house to another. Camden Town, sandwiched between the railway concentrations of Euston Road and Kentish Town, was overwhelmed by their presence and side-effects. So that while in the 1860s Camden Town could be described as being 'a rapidly improving area where first class business may be done' it was also, after the demolition of the slums of Agar Town, an area which had a 'great influx of the lower classes'.

It is not surprising that prostitution was part of the underground world of Camden Town. As early as 1867 the number of 'over-dressed servant girls heading south on Sundays' for the Haymarket, off Piccadilly, (a red-light district then), was being commented on. Streets near Regent's Park were used for encounters of an unmentionable kind, and illegitimacy and infanticide were on the increase. In 1866 the local coroner said that in one year he had held inquests on eighty children found dead in the streets, and he believed there were many more buried secretly.

This *demi-monde* reputation of Camden Town was enhanced by the murder of Emily Dimmock, a part-time prostitute, in Agar Grove in 1907. It was one of those murders which caught the avid curiosity of the public – there was nothing particularly remarkable about the crime, but the public felt a *frisson* as evidence unfolded of the murky and unpublicised night life of Camden Town and its southern hinterland. Even allowing for a good deal of patronising inventiveness in a recent book on the case, it is clear that from Euston Road northwards and southwards an underworld existed, of pubs which unaccompanied women used, of decrepit lodging houses used for prostitution, of a desperate section of society whose sex precluded them from legitimately earning enough to survive in the capital.

A colourful description of the area is contained in *Sinister Street* by Compton Mackenzie. Describing a journey of the principal character, the author writes: 'When the cab had crossed the junction of the Euston Road with the Tottenham Court Road, un-

130. *St Paul's Road* (now Agar Grove) *c*1905.

St. Paul's Road, Camden Square, N. W.

Daily Mirror

THE MORNING JOURNAL WITH THE SECOND LARGEST NET SALE.

See To-day's 'DAILY MAIL.'

No. 1,286. Registered at the G.P.O. as a Newspaper. FRIDAY, DECEMBER 13, 1907. One Halfpenny.

CAMDEN TOWN MURDER MYSTERY: ROBERT WOOD ON TRIAL FOR HIS LIFE AT THE NEW BAILEY.

The curtain rose on the third act in the Camden Town murder drama yesterday when Robert Wood, an artist, was put in the dock at the Central Criminal Court and tried for the murder of Emily Dimmock on the night of September 11. (1) Robert Wood, the accused man. (2) Emily Dimmock, the murdered woman. (3) Ruby Young, the accused man's sweetheart, who is the principal witness for the prosecution. (4) Mr. Marshall Hall, the leading counsel for the defence. (5) Mr. Arthur Newton, the prisoner's solicitor, who prepared the defence, and who defended Wood during the magisterial hearing. (6) The crowd outside the New Bailey watching the entrance of Ruby Young, who is under one of the umbrellas seen in the photograph. (7) Mr. Justice Grantham, the presiding Judge. (8) Sir Charles Mathews, who is prosecuting on behalf of the Crown. (Elliott and Fry, Gresswell, Bassano, and London Stereoscopic.)

131. The *Daily Mirror* front page of the Dimmock murder case in 1907.

known London with all its sly and labyrinthine romance lured his fancy onwards. Maple's and Shoolbred's, those outposts of shopping civilisation, were left behind, and the Hampstead Road with a hint of roguery began.' At a bridge at Camden Town 'The hansom clattered through the murk beneath, past the dim people huddled upon the pavement, past a wheel-barrow and the obscene skeletons and outlines of humanity chalked upon the arches of sweating brick…He caught sight of a slop-shop where old clothes smothered the entrance with their mucid heaps and, just beyond, of three houses from whose surface the stucco was peeling in great scabs and the damp was oozing in livid arabesques and scrawls of verdigris.'

One should not take too literally this fevered description by an author whose imagination took flight at the existence of a way of life so alien to him, and from which he had been carefully preserved, but his words conjure up a sleazy, smoky, decaying Camden Town that probably existed. Certainly, old photographs of the area, confirm that the place was in decline, and certainly prostitution was rife. One need look no further than the matter-of-fact pages of the vestry minutes to see that the trade had been going on for some time. In 1889 it was reported that the police were doing their best to deal with the matter of prostitutes in Camden Road. Among those disorderly houses reported in the 1880s some were in Camden Street, Ampthill Place, Rousden Street, St Mark's Crescent and Gloucester Avenue. In 1905 in the space of four days, 41 couples entered and left, after a short time, an address in Park Village East.

132. Local bus tickets which bring instantly to mind, to those who are old enough, the little machines that conductors carried to punch holes in the tickets.

AN UNDERGROUND RAILWAY

Even more reason for finding a cheap room in Camden Town was the building of the underground railway from the West End of London. The Charing Cross, Euston and Hampstead Railway, or the Hampstead Tube as it was called, was opened on 22 June, 1907. The title was not exact, for at Camden Town the line forked and also went up to what is now Archway station.

The opening ceremony was performed by David Lloyd George at what was then the country terminus of Golders Green, and after 1pm London in general was invited to try the system out – 127,000 of them did on the first day. It created, the proprietors said, the opportunity to live in the country (meaning Golders Green, Highgate and Hampstead), but it also ensured that Camden Town was easy to get to from the West End, and when the City branch of the Northern line was constructed in 1924, Camden Town assumed even more importance.

The area was reasonably well served by trams, but none went from Camden to Kentish Town. Presumably either the railway bridge over Kentish Town Road, by Camden Gardens, was too low, or else the bridge over the canal was too weak, because a straight route between the two centres was an obvious attraction. Instead, the trams went up Chalk Farm Road, turned into Ferdinand Street and up to South End Green – there was a tram shed in Cressy Road. By 1911 the main bus company, the London General, had only one omnibus, the no. 24, along the High Street, although two routes came up Albany Street. There were no buses along Royal College Street or St Pancras Way, and none, according to the 1911 map, along Camden Road, which was tram territory.

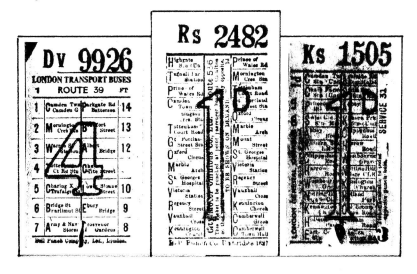

133. A perspective view of the Hampstead Tube, opened in 1907.

THE PROBLEMS OF MORNINGTON CRESCENT

Mornington Crescent began with a splendid rear view. Before the railway came an estate agent could have said, with justification, that there was little between the Crescent and Regent's Park, other than the decorative spur of the Regent's Canal. The railway changed all that, bringing not only a reduced social status and the transition of the houses into cheap lodging places, of the sort delighted in by Sickert, but also, later, some model dwellings built by the railway company itself to rehouse those it had displaced.

The final indignity was the loss of the gardens in front. A developer bought up all the garden rights of the houses and then on the patch of green erected for Carreras 'the most modern hygienic cigarette factory in the world'. This opened in November 1928. The impunity with which this block was planted on green space sparked off considerable controversy and a tightening up of planning regulations in London. But such is the whim of fashion that in the early 1960s, when the building was being transformed into the faceless office block that it now

is, there were cries that this pseudo-Egyptian building should be desecrated so. Readers unfamiliar with its appearance then should look at the Hoover factory on the A40, which has similar detail and colouring, but in the case of the Carreras factory, designed by M.E. and O.H. Collins in a style fashionable since the opening of Tutankhamen's tomb, there were also two large black cats outside, indicating the brand name of the most popular Carreras cigarette. Behind the building still is a chimney masquerading as an Egyptian obelisk.

134. *Mornington Crescent c1905.*

135. *The Carreras factory*, an illustration issued by the Company to advertise its new factory at Mornington Crescent.

CARRERAS LIMITED EST? 1788 LONDON

CARRERAS

...TE FACTORY IN THE WORLD

...ETTE FACTORY
...DUCTIONS OF
...IMITED
...NT CIGARETTE MANUFACTURERS

OUTRAGE AND MUSIC IN REGENT'S PARK ROAD

The residents of Regent's Park Road and Gloucester Avenue achieved a remarkably easy victory against a building proposal in 1905. In those days the local authority had rather less powers than it has now and if someone wished to pull down a mansion and replace it with smaller houses, or a block of flats, then they could without too much trouble.

That year the London & North Western Railway, obliged to rehouse people from houses it was demolishing in the Euston area, proposed to knock down two large houses at the junction of Regent's Park Road and Gloucester Avenue. These twin Italianate villas, each with a tower, faced majestically out towards Parkway. The plan of the railway company was to replace them with workmen's dwellings, of the kind they had already built near Mornington Crescent.

The protesters were successful within two weeks, when the railway company scrapped the plan. The most likely reason for this speedy victory was that the LNWR required the approval of the Council for a development Bill going through Parliament and St Pancras declined to give it until the Regent's Park Road plan was dropped.

In the event the houses were taken in the late 1920s by the English Folk Dance Society who built on their site, in 1930, the present neo-Georgian Cecil Sharp House, designed by H.M. Fletcher (though it was one storey less when opened). The recent furore over whether the English Folk Dance and Song Society should vacate and sell this building has been of much longer duration than the 1905 battle.

136. *Cecil Sharp House*, Regent's Park Road.

MUNICIPAL STIRRINGS

St Pancras Council and the Vestry which preceded it were careful with ratepayers' money and as a consequence they edged slowly into municipal provision of facilities. Yet in one area they were leaders, and that was the supply of electricity. Both in Stanhope Street and between St Pancras Way and Royal College Street the Vestry built, in the early 1890s, electricity stations that were to be the first owned and run by a local authority in London. It was a bold venture, considering the complexity of electricity supply, but the Vestry had had too many problems with the private gas supply companies to want a repetition in the supply of this amazing new power.

St Pancras Council was slow off the mark in providing municipal housing. It was not until 1904 that Goldington Buildings (now Court) was built on the site of a timber yard and the Elephant & Castle pub. But judging from the turn-out on the opening day the councillors were quite proud of themselves; they would be pleased to see their first project now renovated and with splendid new gates.

Even slower had been the adoption of the Act to provide free libraries in St Pancras. Under the rules governing vestries it had been required to call a local referendum to vote on the adoption of the Act and each time the voters (which was not at that time the whole adult population) turned the proposal down. The Council, which followed the Vestry in 1899, and was run by 'Progressives', was under no such limitation. By 1904 the Act had been adopted and in 1906 the first public library in the borough was opened – at Chester Road, Highgate. But it was not until 1921 that another municipal library appeared, this time in a converted house – no. 18 Camden Street. This 'temporary' branch lasted until 1964, when it was replaced by the present building in Camden High Street.

137. *The opening of Goldington Buildings*, at the junction of Royal College Street and St Pancras Way, in 1904, the first municipal homes in St Pancras.

138. *Camden Town Library*, 18 Camden Street. Until modern times the library buildings provided by St Pancras Borough were among the worst in London. Only one purpose-built library existed – in Highgate New Town. All the others were in quite unsuitable, converted houses, such as the one illustrated here, which was used from 1920 until 1964.

139. Camden Town was not without its Drill Hall. The 17th North Middlesex Rifle Volunteers had their headquarters at 74–76 Camden High Street. The personalities at the opening ceremony are depicted here.

OPENING OF THE NEW DRILL HALL OF THE 17TH NORTH MIDDLESEX RIFLES.

140. *Camden Town* in the 1920s

141. The opening of a new bridge over the canal in St Pancras Way, in July 1897.

More Modern Times

TOO MANY WHEELS

The weight of traffic through Camden Town has been a problem much of this century. Old pictures of the High Street show that the horse-drawn vehicles were quite often as congested as today's motor cars. In the very year that the underground was opened at Camden Town, 1907, local residents sent a petition to the Home Secretary asking him to devise a way of relieving the district of the heavy motor traffic through the area. The difference now, of course, is that the minor roads of Bayham, Camden and Royal College Streets are also overrun by vehicles, and fast vehicles at that.

In the 1970s a tidy solution to the north London traffic problem was proposed – the Motorway Box. Linked to the M1 extension, the six-lane highway would run from near Kilburn station to York Way and, in addition, a spur would go south from the Camden goods yard behind the back of Camden High Street, roughly over the Euston-bound railway. This proposal of the Greater London Council was judged for what it was – one of benefit to the motorist and of disadvantage to the resident.

The scheme met some articulate opposition – one does not run a road through Hampstead and Camden Town with impunity. It was this argued hostility, the gradual realisation by the GLC that such a brutalist solution was inappropriate, and the fact that it would have been far too expensive, that led to the plan's defeat. But it was a near-run thing at the time.

142. The Camden Town section of the Motorway Box goes horizontally across the map, while its spur, the Camden Town by-pass, goes south.

THE IRISH IN CAMDEN TOWN

The Irish and Camden Town have been synonymous for many years, and though other nationalities appear now to be more predominant the Irish population is still the most numerous of the immigrants. How did this concentration of Irish in Camden Town come about?

Most likely the earliest Irish settlement in London was in the St Giles-in-the-Fields area in the 16th century. They came for seasonal unskilled work, such as harvesting, and stayed to become itinerant costermongers or else went into building work. The clearance of the St Giles rookeries in the mid–19th century forced the unfortunate inhabitants northwards, some to Agar Town (see p64) and many to the growing Camden and Somers Towns. Both these latter places provided not only cheap housing but also they were near to the railways which were primarily built and serviced by the Irish. Kilburn,

with its vast railway lands, was another favoured place.

In the 19th century Engels had little regard for the Irish. He thought them 'the sorest evil [England] has to deal with' and remarked on how the position of the English worker 'has been still more degraded by the presence of Irish competition'.

But continual economic problems in Ireland and the extraordinary growth of industry in England which required cheap and strong labour ensured that the Irish kept on coming. Even more recently when governments have been stricter in the matter, the British have allowed the unrestricted entry of Irish men into this country because their labour was needed. Unfortunately, many men come over poor, are badly paid when they get here, bring no family with them, and find it hard to get either accommodation or comfort. This has generally been their lot in Camden Town and it is hard to see any improvement in the near future.

143. *Manley Street* in the 1970s. These cottages for railway workers are now demolished.

144. Damage to Camden Town in the 2nd World War was surprisingly light. Here, in a 1940 picture, an empty bus has been blown against a house in Harrington Square.

145. Camden Town Underground Station was hit by a bomb in 1941.

THE GREEK CYPRIOTS

No convincing reason has been suggested for the concentration of Greek Cypriots in Camden Town other than that the large influx since the 1960s merely camped where the earliest settlement had taken root. The first groups came in the 1930s to escape the poverty of Cyprus and, just like the Irish, it was the men who came, and who sent money back home. They worked mainly in the restaurants of Soho and the hotels of the West End. Perhaps Camden Town was merely the most convenient place to be. After the war they were to be found managing food shops and later they took to fast-food places, springing on the conservative English the kebab restaurants and then, final indignity, taking over and generally improving the fish and chip shops.

Whatever the reason for the initial choice, the large influx of the late 1950s and early 1960s had of necessity to begin with relations already in Camden Town. Quite often this new wave consisted of young married couples and it was they who were able to set up the family-operated groceries, off-licences and shoe-mending and clothes-making businesses which now are familiar in much of north London. On the whole they did not go into the newsagency trade which is now almost entirely run by immigrants from the Indian sub-continent.

A third wave of Greek Cypriots came to Camden Town after the Turkish occupation of the northern part of Cyprus in 1974.

The two communities, the Irish and the Greek Cypriots, have one feature in common – a religious life now quite unusual in the indigenous population (the Anglican parish church of Camden Town usually has a congregation below double figures each Sunday). All Saints Church is the centre of the Greek community in Camden Town – congregations are large, as indeed they are up the road in Kentish Town at St Andrew's, and all marriages take place in church – a registered wedding without a church ceremony is unthinkable.

146. The immediate post-war years. A flank wall in Camden Street in 1945, complete with election poster.

147. The junction of Royal College Street and Camden Road, 1945. Traffic is almost non-existent, advertisements abound, and Ferodo already rule supreme on railway bridges.

DREAMS AT THE ROUNDHOUSE

There is something very alluring about buildings of the industrial age, with their mixture of iron and brick. The Roundhouse, once it had been emptied of bottles and left derelict, has been no exception, and it became available at a time when 'theatre-in-the-round', a return to the common theatre of Shakespeare's time, was the latest fashion.

In September 1960 the Trades Union Congress passed Resolution 42 calling for greater participation by the Trade Union movement in all cultural activities. This proposal, though bland, was unusual at the annual conference since it concerned art and not industrial or political matters. But it was taken seriously by a group of people whose ideal was that art, so far as possible, should be free and more accessible to the community. More particularly they lighted upon the Roundhouse in the Chalk Farm Road as a perfect venue for this new dawn, a building in which all the art forms could be seen and relate to each other.

In retrospect one can be sceptical about the proposal, but it was a time, thank goodness, when ideals were taken seriously. A lease of the building was obtained and the playwright, Arnold Wesker, became its director. He was backed by a council and a group of Friends who included all the great and the good of left-wing politics.

It seemed like a new beginning in the arts, but it was not to be. Enthusiasm and funds declined, the trade union movement did not put its own resolution very high in its priorities, and eventually Wesker left. The building then entered into a new phase in which visiting companies used the auditorium, and the Roundhouse began to attract critical acclaim as a venue. The freehold was obtained, a Downstairs Theatre built, a commercial building erected next door to provide income, and all seemed set fair again even if it was not quite as originally intended.

But again it was not to be. The cost of maintaining and improving the building escalated beyond what grants and receipts could cover, and eventually The Roundhouse closed. It had been a brave attempt and it was a dignified exit.

The empty building inspired a new dream, this time of a Black Arts Centre. Enormous sums of money were poured into the creation of a unique venue but despite the public money this plan came to an ignominious end.

There are now other plans in the air, equally as grandiose. The lure of an interior designed to allow the servicing of small railway engines seems not yet to have run out of steam.

EXTRAVAGANZAS ON THE CANAL

Two extraordinary buildings may be seen from the towpath of the Regent's Canal at Camden Town.

One is the Pirate's Castle, a mock medieval castle designed by the ubiquitous Seifert and Partners. This was opened in October 1977 to serve as the headquarters of the Pirate Club, founded by Viscount St Davids in 1966, to provide boating and canoeing for children.

The second is the TV-am building, which fronts on to Hawley Crescent. On the site previously had been the Camden Brewery and afterwards a Henley garage. The TV-am building, designed by the Terry Farrell Partnership in 1982, is an extravaganza of pipes, complete with boiled eggs on the roof. Quite what this building would be used for if the television company lost its franchise, is an interesting thought, but let us hope that the eggs will remain as a piece of industrial archaeology to remind future Camden Town people of the 1980s.

148. An empty Roundhouse building after Gilbey's had left.

149. *Pirate's Castle* on the Regent's Canal.

NEW PEOPLE IN CAMDEN TOWN

'Gentrification', whatever its social consequences, has preserved the housing stock of whole swathes of London. In the 1960s and 1970s middle-class couples, many of them of working class origin without the cushion of private income or the prospect of inheritance, decided to take on the crumbling terraces of Islington, Fulham, Kentish Town and Camden Town. To the surprise of their parents, who had moved to such sanitary safe-havens as Becontree and Billericay, their university-educated offspring voluntarily immersed themselves in the grimy urban terraces that they had themselves escaped from.

We should be grateful to the incomers, for without them we would now have as many 1960s curtain wall blocks as the local councils could have afforded. Tower Hamlets is testimony to what happened when an open cheque book met no opposition.

The gestation period of council development is a long one and schemes of the mid–1960s were often the product of planning in the 1950s. By 1965 Cam-

den councillors were fully aware of the awful drawbacks of earlier schemes and it was evident that in many instances saving and renovating the handsome terraces was probably a better solution to the housing problem than full-scale redevelopment in estates. However, it was too late to reverse a programme which had been formulated at least ten years previously. Utopia may be hard to achieve, but it is also expensive to arrest. It was with many misgivings, therefore, that the eastern side of Oakley Square was destroyed to build an estate which most distinctly is no ornament to the area and, indeed, hides itself away from the gardens it overlooks.

Even worse occurred nearby. The three disastrous tower blocks (now in new clothes) which herald the arrival of Camden Town at Mornington Crescent, had been planned and designed in the 1950s, but for reasons to do with the purchase of the site detailed consideration of the development did not occur until the late 1960s. By then, laymen, if not planners, of any sense were opposed to tower blocks because it was known that apart from the difficulties of living in them, especially with children, they achieved only a small housing gain and

150. *A villa on Primrose Hill Road.* The Victorian villas and houses on Primrose Hill Road have now been replaced by blocks of flats which, given their prime site, are dismal successors.

were atrociously expensive to maintain. Councillors, presented with plans for the three towers that showed blocks in traditional 'Stalinist' style, turned them down and preferred to think anew; they were, however, advised that if the scheme and the architect were thrown out they, the councillors, could be liable to individual surcharge for wasting ratepayers' money. It will probably be forty years before this serious mistake can be rectified.

The Council had, however, made some successful forays into the buying up and renovation of terraces, notably to the east of Camden High Street, and in Kentish Town, though these now look beaten down a bit from neglect and traffic. And, it should be said, a great deal of thought went into the design of the two estates between Bayham and Royal College Streets, in one of which the Camden Studios were rebuilt (see p83).

Gloucester Crescent and Albert Street led the gentrification movement in Camden Town, a social phenomenon captured accurately in Alan Bennett's NW1 parodies. And then, as the smoke from the railway ceased to enfold the area, so renovation in Chalk Farm spread from the grander houses of Regent's Park Road and Chalcot Square. The advent of conservation areas and the end of the era of municipal redevelopment, have made this physical regeneration safe for the time being. What has been lost is rented accommodation in private houses of the sort which suited impecunious students and others who, for various reasons, could afford a rent but not to buy.

151. *Chalcot Crescent* at the beginning of 'gentrification'.

CHANGES IN THE HIGH STREET

There has been a retailing revolution in Camden Town in the last ten years. Bastions of the old High Street have fallen or have been outpaced. Bowman's and the Co-op have departed, Woolworth's has lost its pivotal attraction, and Marks and Spencer's is too small. Attention has shifted northwards to Camden Lock and east to Sainsbury's.

In the early 1970s the area of Camden Lock was still blighted by the possibility that the Motorway Box would be built across the site. There was little that the new owners could do in the long-term, but as a temporary measure a market, based on craft goods, was begun. Restaurants and bars were added. By the time the motorway was abandoned in 1976 the Lock had established itself as a major attraction. Especially at weekends it became a Mecca for tourists and young people and it was beginning to be uncomfortably crowded.

Redevelopment of the site has now taken place.

On Chalk Farm Road a new and dignified Market Hall has arisen – it was opened in 1991. Designed by John Dickinson, it has inside much splendid iron-work, all newly-made by Colin Appleton of Bruce & Hyslop. Included also is an 'events space' usable for functions and exhibitions. Elsewhere, new buildings have been 'infilled' and it is now difficult to tell which are old and which are new. So far, so good, and it is a credit to both the developers, Northside UK, and the architect. So many people now shop there that the managers of the Underground station complain, on the grounds of safety, at the number of visitors, and threaten closure of the station at weekends instead of devising ways of coping with the influx.

It remains to be seen if the traditional and local clientele of the Lock will find that the new shops are too up-market for them, a bit too Covent Garden or Fulham Road. Will it become the haunt almost exclusively of tourists? We must hope not. And, if only the proprietors of the Lock could get to grips

152. *Camden Lock* in the period before the market was established.

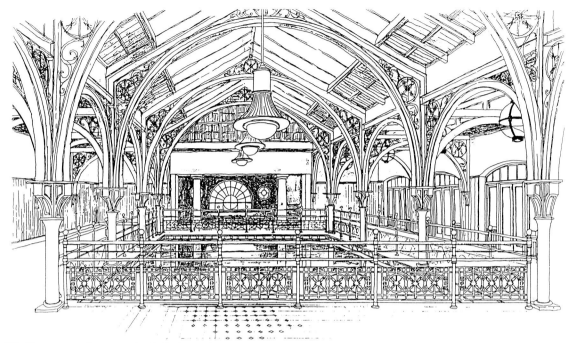

153. The proposed new market hall of Camden Lock, designed by John Dickinson, which opened in 1991. The design for the ironwork has been slightly altered since this drawing was made.

with the litter their patrons leave in their attractive grounds all day, then the place would be a decided asset.

Chalk Farm Road has changed as well. Market stalls are spreading along it and at weekends this end of Camden Town is one of the busiest in London. In the 1960s and 1970s a second-hand furniture specialisation occupied much of Chalk Farm Road, but this is now being pressed hard by shops selling more ephemeral items. At the time of writing the overwhelming brick wall which bounded the old goods yard has been breached at last and Camden Town can look forward to reclaiming that side of the street.

On the corner of Parkway and Camden High Street development looms, but as yet its nature is still uncertain. Both cinemas will be involved, as will the old Co-op building, in a new complex of shopping and leisure. This will, presumably be followed by rebuilding on the other side of the road on the Bowman's site.

Along Camden Road a large Sainsbury's has been built. This attracts architectural students and plaudits, but others think it is the least sensitive

modern building in Camden Town. In particular its rear end facing Kentish Town Road has all the charm of the back of a football stadium.

Parkway has progressively gone up-market as has the enclave of shops in Regent's Park Road. If only a few more estate agents can be persuaded that there isn't enough business to be viable, even more shops could be freed for retail trade. The shops in Parkway now reflect the traditional difference between that street and the High Street, evident as long as a hundred years ago. While the High Street was, and still is, a place for essentials, Parkway is a place for leisure and ornament. If it were possible to do away with Parkway's traffic, fill it with cobbles, ornamental bollards and pot plants and all the other paraphernalia assumed necessary for pedestrian precincts, then it would become very prosperous indeed.

It is most likely that if new shopping developments are handled wisely Camden Town will become once again a principal retail centre for north London. In so doing it will threaten even more the well-being of shops in Kentish Town and Holloway.

INDEX

Entries in bold type indicate
illustrations.